REMEMBER LOT'S WIFE

REMEMBER LOT'S WIFE

Scriptural Reflections on
How to Lose Your Life and Save It

MARTIN J. BURNE, OSB

ST PAULS

Library of Congress Cataloging-in-Publication Data

Burne, Martin J., 1914-2003.
    Remember Lot's wife : scriptural reflections on how to lose your life and save it /
Martin J. Burne.
        p. cm.
    ISBN 13: 978-0-8189-1241-2 (alk. paper)
    ISBN 10: 0-8189-1241-3 (alk. paper)
1. Christian life—Biblical teaching. 2. Bible—Meditations.   I. Title.

BS680.C47B87 2007
242'.5—dc22

2006032003

Produced and designed in the United States of America by the
Fathers and Brothers of the Society of St. Paul,
2187 Victory Boulevard, Staten Island, New York 10314-6603,
as part of their communications apostolate.

ISBN-13: 978-0-8189-1241-2
ISBN-10: -0-8189-1241-3

Printing Information:

Current Printing - first digit   1   2   3   4   5   6   7   8   9   10

Year of Current Printing - first year shown

2007   2008   2009   2010   2011   2012   2013   2014   2015   2016

DEDICATION

Dedicated to the women religious
whose contribution to the Church in the United States
through their teaching, nursing and other ministries
is beyond measure.

TABLE OF CONTENTS

Foreword (Rt. Rev. Giles P. Hayes, OSB,
Abbot of St. Mary's Abbey) ix

Preface xiii

1. Remember Lot's Wife 1
2. Whose Daughter Are You? 7
3. He Laughs 13
4. Lord We Have Sinned 19
5. I Will Show You the Man You Seek 25
6. Elected By God 33
7. You Are the Man 39
8. The Mastic and the Oak 47
9. Is the Arm of God Short? 53
10. Roaming the Earth and Patrolling It 59
11. I Will Say What My God Tells Me 65
12. I Will Make a New Covenant 71
13. I Was No Prophet 79
14. I Will Lead Her Into the Desert 85
15. Mene, Tekel, Peres 93
16. The Infancy Narratives 101

17. The Kingdom of Heaven Is at Hand 109

18. Go to Siloam and Wash 115

19. Unexhausted Favors 121

20. To Walk With Jesus 127

21. Words From the Cross 133

22. On the Third Day 139

23. Woman, Why Are You Weeping? 145

24. Were Not Our Hearts Burning? 151

25. I Will Be Their Shepherd 157

26. Consenting to His Execution 165

FOREWORD

ectio Divina, a prayerful, meditative reading of sacred scripture, has been practiced by Christians, especially monks, nuns and religious, since before the time of sixth century St. Benedict. Because an individual encounters Christ in the reading of sacred scripture, those who practice Lectio Divina come to know Him and His Father intimately. This process results in the disciple becoming facile with the use of sacred scripture and growing more generous, warm, considerate of others, and self-sacrificing in every way. Indeed, the faithful practice of Lectio Divina helps make one another Christ.

This book is a result of a disciple of the Lord's Lectio Divina over many years. The author, Abbot Martin J. Burne, O.S.B., was a saintly spiritual master and an important leader of the American Church in the second half of the twentieth century. Abbot Martin died on July 25, 2003. The monks of St. Mary's Abbey, Abbot Martin's community for 68 years, are publishing his book.

Born in December, 1914, in Irvington, New Jersey, Abbot Martin was graduated from St. Benedict's Preparatory School, Newark, in 1932; professed vows as a member of St. Mary's Abbey in July, 1935; was ordained to the priesthood in May, 1940; and became a chaplain in the United States Navy in 1942. After serving with the Marines in Guadalcanal, Bougainville, and Guam, he was honorably discharged in 1946. While he was a faithful monk and had attended to sacred scripture before the Second World War, he often said that his military career made him even more faithful to Lectio Divina. In 1944, for example, he began the practice, continued until death, of reading sacred scripture, one page after another, from Genesis to the Apocalypse, for a minimum of 45 minutes a day over and over again.

Abbot Martin returned to St. Benedict's where he taught German and music, earning a doctorate in music from New York University in 1956. He became sub-prior at St. Mary's Abbey at that time, prior in 1958, and novice master from 1963-1966. In that year he was elected the fifth abbot of St. Mary's, which position he held until 1971, when he became President of the American-Cassinese Congregation. He taught at Immaculate Conception Seminary, served as director of liturgy in the Diocese of Paterson, as administrator of Holy Cross Abbey in Colorado, and regularly taught speech and religion at Delbarton School from 1965 until he retired in 1995.

To all who knew him, Abbot Martin's extraordinary leadership of the Benedictines resulted from his daily encounters with Christ and the Father through scripture. More than that, it resulted as well in his passionate concern about those in his care, the monks of St. Mary's Abbey and Newark Abbey, but also of those suffering anywhere, particularly from injustice, racism, poverty, anti-Semitism, and violence. He was an active disciple of Martin Luther King, Jr., and followed him on a number of his marches. A regional spokesman for civil rights in New Jersey, Abbot Martin was positioned right up front during the March on Washington of August, 1963. Most importantly for not only the Benedictines in New Jersey but also the poor, he played a major role in designating Newark Abbey as an independent entity in 1968, and in setting the goals of the Newark community towards serving the people of Newark right where they were on Martin Luther King Boulevard. In part, because of his influence and vision, Newark Abbey now conducts one of the most significant urban independent schools in America.

Happily, this writer, and his monastic classmate, Abbot Melvin J. Valvano, O.S.B., the second Abbot of Newark Abbey, both enjoyed the friendship and the spiritual direction of Abbot Martin for many years of their adult monastic lives. Indeed, dozens of us in Newark and Morristown were so blessed, and all of us had the benefit of his wise instruction in homilies and conferences, of his gentle but firm leadership, of his total concern for each one of us and even for our extended families, of his courtesy, and of the example of his humility. In a word, he was Christ to us.

Abbot Martin loved the Hebrew Scriptures. He knew that Christ himself derived his own nourishment from reading them, the Prophets especially, and everything handed down to Him from the tradition. In reading the Hebrew Scriptures, the Old Testament, Abbot Martin knew that he would find Christ there and that he would be more deeply transformed into Him. May you, the reader, benefit the same way from Abbot Martin's reflection.

Rt. Rev. Giles P. Hayes, OSB
Abbot, St. Mary's Abbey, Morristown, New Jersey
August, 2006

PREFACE

In the course of his instruction on the Day of the Son of Man, Jesus urges those listening to "remember Lot's wife." He adds at once: "Whoever seeks to preserve his life will lose it, but whoever loses it will save it." The meditations at hand endeavor to illustrate our Savior's admonition.

1

REMEMBER LOT'S WIFE

e are indebted to the Gospel of Luke for the three simple words, "Remember Lot's wife," that take us back to Sodom and Gomorrah. We cannot know, however, to what Jesus was referring when he spoke those words unless we go back and review the story told in Genesis, a story that unveils the problems surrounding the two cities whose names have become infamous over the centuries.

Because events narrated in the first eleven chapters of Genesis are largely undatable, that section of Sacred Scripture is often spoken of as pre-history. Toward the latter part of the eleventh chapter, however, the sacred writer undertakes to trace the record of the descendants of Shem, son of Noah. Subsequently the ancestry of Abraham (spoken of at first as Abram) is introduced through his father Terah, and Abram is spoken of as having two brothers, Nahor and Haran, the last of whom is the father of Lot. When, a bit later, we are told that Terah had moved from Ur of the Chaldees to Haran, in the Fertile Crescent, the text reads: "Terah took his son Abram, his grandson Lot, son of Haran, and his daughter-in-law Sarai, the wife of his son Abram, and brought them out of Ur of the Chaldeans, to go to the land of Canaan. But when they reached Haran, they settled there" (Genesis 11:31).

When Abram is called by God to leave Haran for a land that God will show him, we are told that "Abram took his wife Sarai, his brother's son Lot, all the possessions that they had accumulated, and the persons they had acquired in Haran, and they set out for the land of Canaan" (Genesis 12:5). Genesis makes no mention of Lot accompanying Sarai and Abram when famine conditions prompt them to leave Canaan for Egypt, but when the couple leave Egypt we are told: "From Egypt Abram went up to the Negeb with his wife and all that belonged to him, and Lot accompanied him" (Genesis 13:1). It is at this juncture that we learn of the extensive flocks and herds and tents that both Abram and Lot have, so that the land is unable to support them together. Abram then bids Lot to choose whatever land he will: "If you prefer the left, I will go to the right; if you prefer the right, I will go to the left" (Genesis 12:10). Lot, seeing how well-watered the Jordan Plain was, set out eastward, separating from Abram, pitching his tent near Sodom.

At a later date a battle ensues between small groups of kings (or petty chieftains), and in the course of events the victors carried off possessions and food supplies from Sodom and Gomorrah, taking with them Lot and his possessions. When word reached Abram, he mustered his retainers and went in pursuit, defeated those who had captured Lot, bringing back his nephew and his possessions, along with the women and other captives. This is the last we hear of Lot in the Genesis account until the Lord apprises Abraham (his name has now been changed) that because of the wickedness of Sodom and Gomorrah, the two cities are about to be destroyed. Abraham intercedes for the cities, asking God if he will destroy the cities if fifty innocent people can be found there. The Lord assures the patriarch that if fifty innocent people can be found in the city of Sodom, he will not destroy the city. Abraham, you will recall, presses the Lord, reducing the number fifty ulti-mately to ten. "The Lord departed as soon as he had finished speak-ing with Abraham, and Abraham returned home" (Genesis 18:33).

It is at this point in the Genesis story that Lot comes into prominence as two angels enter the city of Sodom while Lot is sit-ting at the gate of the city. According to a long-standing tradition at the time in the East, a city's residents were expected to welcome strangers, particularly when they arrive at eventide and seem to have no particular host to welcome them. Lot's behavior accords with the tradition: "When Lot saw them, he got up to greet them; and bowing down with his face to the ground, he said, 'Please, gentlemen, come aside into your servant's house for the night, and bathe your feet; you can get up early to continue your journey'" (Genesis 19:1-2). The angels at first refused Lot's invitation, but upon his urging them they acquiesced. A meal was prepared for the guests, and they dined.

Before the guests retired, all the townsmen of Sodom came to Lot's house, insisting that he turn out the two guests in order that the townsmen might have intimacies with them. So great was their insistence that the angels pulled Lot inside with them, and closed the door. "At the same time they struck the men at the en-trance of the house, one and all, with such a blinding light that they were utterly unable to reach the doorway" (Genesis 19:11). The guests then let Lot know that they are about to destroy Sodom and tell their host to get out of the city with his wife, daughters and sons-in-law to be. When Lot tried to convey the message to the latter, they thought that he was joking and refused to leave. At dawn the angels urge Lot on: "On your way! Take with you your wife and your two daughters who are here, or you will be swept away in the punishment of the city" (Genesis 19:15).

It is always possible, in reading any part of the Sacred Scriptures, to allow our attention to focus on those aspects of life that do not edify us and to neglect, in those same Scriptures, areas that can serve to improve no end our living out of the Christian Gospel. In the Abraham-Lot account so far considered, we think of the generosity of Abraham in permitting his nephew to select whatever land he would for pasturing his flocks and for his dwelling. The concern of the patriarch again comes to light as Abraham rescues Lot and the latter's possessions. And when we read of Abraham interceding in behalf of Sodom, we cannot but be impressed by a kind of selflessness worthy of our reflection. But it is not simply the conduct of the patriarch that is highlighted in the sacred text. Lot's solicitude for the two strangers whom he meets at the city gate reminds us of a gospel value emphasized time and again in the New Testament. How vital that we read the Hebrew Scriptures with one eye on our own lives, seeking ways that those lives can be enhanced through our contemplation of what we read.

Commentators on Saint Luke's Gospel sometimes speak of the evangelist's "travel narrative," an account that is divided into three sections and that shows Jesus' progress toward Jerusalem. The third such section, which like the first and second is an instruction on the meaning of the Christian Way, begins with Luke's seventeenth chapter, wherein we read: "As he continued his journey to Jerusalem, he traveled through Samaria and Galilee" (Luke 17:11). Jesus cleanses ten lepers whom he encounters, and in reply to a question placed by the Pharisees, our Savior says: "The kingdom of God is among you." Now comes an extended section that speaks of the days of the Son of Man:

> Then he said to his disciples, "The days will come when you will long to see one of the days of the Son of Man, but you will not see it. There will be those who will say

to you, 'Look, there he is,' or 'Look, here he is.' Do not go off, do not run in pursuit. For just as lightning flashes and lights up the sky from one side to the other, so will the Son of Man be in his day. But first he must suffer greatly and be rejected by this generation."

(Luke 17:22-25)

Jesus then goes on to speak of the days of Noah: People were eating and drinking, paying scant attention to Noah and his building of the ark, when the flood came and destroyed them all. So in the time of Lot: "They were eating, drinking, buying, selling, planting, building; on the day when Lot left Sodom, fire and brimstone rained from the sky to destroy them all. So it will be on the day when the Son of Man is revealed" (Luke 17:28-29). Thus Jesus relates the day of the Son of Man to Lot, urged by the angels to be on his way.

When he hesitated, the men, by the Lord's mercy, seized his hand and the hands of his wife and two daughters and led them to safety outside the city. As soon as they had been brought outside, he was told: "Flee for your life! Don't look back or stop anywhere on the plain. Get off to the hills at once, or you will be swept away."

(Genesis 19:16-17)

Lot asks the angels if he may flee to a town called Zoar instead of trying to make it to the hills. The favor was granted Lot, with an assurance that that town would not be overthrown in the destruction of Sodom and Gomorrah.

The sun was just rising over the earth as Lot arrived in Zoar; at the same time the Lord rained down sulphurous fire upon Sodom and Gomorrah. He overthrew those cities and the whole Plain, together with the inhabitants of the cities and the produce of the soil. But Lot's wife looked back, and she was turned into a pillar of salt. (Genesis 19:23-26)

When, in Saint Luke's Gospel, our Savior continues to describe the coming of the Son of Man, he warns the disciples that on that day "a person who is on the housetop and whose belongings are in the house must not go down to get them, and likewise a person in the field must not return to what was left behind. Remember the wife of Lot" (Luke 17:31-32).

One cannot know for certain what prompted Lot's wife to look back (or turn back), but the clear inference of Jesus is that we must continue to look ahead to the unseen future, trusting the God of deliverance to guide us as God will. To yearn to go back, to fail to appreciate the newness to which God calls us, can be a failure on our part to remember Lot's wife. To move forward, on the contrary, as the Lord bids us, likens us to the pillar of fire (that beckoned God's people to deliverance from their captivity in Egypt) rather than to the pillar of salt: "The Lord preceded them, in the daytime by a column of cloud to show them the way, and at night by means of a column of fire to give them light" (Exodus 13:21).

Each of the meditations in the pages ahead is designed to remind us of the God who calls each of us to the unseen (yet not completely unknown) future. Day by day an all-loving Lord infuses our very beings with grace and asks that we follow his bidding in faith. May each of us accept the invitation given us, hearkening to the message of the Gospel: "Remember Lot's wife!"

2

WHOSE DAUGHTER ARE YOU?

One of the longest stories in the Book of Genesis, almost saga-like, concerns a servant who, despite the length and importance of his mission, remains unnamed throughout. Abraham has reached a ripe old age and is concerned that his son, Isaac, obtain a suitable wife. To this end he calls to himself the senior servant of his household: "Put your hand under my thigh, and I will make you swear by the Lord, the God of heaven and the God of earth, that you will not procure a wife for my son from the daughters of the Canaanites among whom I live, but that you will go to my own land and my kindred to get a wife for my son Isaac" (Genesis 24:2-4). The servant raised just one objection: "What if the woman is unwilling to follow me to this land? Should I then take your son back to the land from which you migrated?" Abraham's reply is unequivocal: "Never take my son back there for any reason." Abraham goes on to assure the servant that if the woman chosen for Isaac refuses to come to Canaan, the servant will be released from his oath. "So the servant put his hand under the thigh of his master Abraham and swore to him in this undertaking" (Genesis 24:9).

Twice in the Book of Genesis is someone asked to place his

hand under the thigh of another: the first is found here as Abraham bids his servant travel back to the "old country" to find a wife for Isaac; the second instance occurs later when Jacob, near to death, begs his son Joseph not to bury him in Egypt, but to bury him in Canaan with his ancestors. The expression, "put your hand under my thigh," is not used lightly: only for very serious or even grave matters is the custom invoked, a custom based on the understanding that sons came from a father's thigh, really here a euphemism for the male organ; the man who took such an oath was perhaps believed to incur sterility if the oath were not carried out.

The "saga" now begins. The servant takes ten of his master's camels and all kinds of gifts and begins his journey. Interestingly, little or nothing is said of events along the way. In a matter of seconds, it seems, the servant is outside the area in which Abraham's kin live, and it is now that the special character of the servant begins to unveil itself.

> Near evening, at the time when women go out to draw water, he made the camels kneel by the well outside the city. Then he prayed: "Lord, God of my master Abraham, let it turn out favorably for me today and thus deal graciously with my master Abraham. While I stand here at the spring and the daughters of the townsmen are coming out to draw water, if I say to a girl, 'Please lower your jug, that I may drink,' and she answers, 'Take a drink, and let me give water to your camels, too,' let her be the one whom you have decided upon for your servant Isaac. In this way I shall know that you have dealt graciously with my master."   (Genesis 24:11-14)

Hardly had he completed his prayer when Rebecca came out with a jug on her shoulder. Sacred Scripture at once identifies her:

she is the daughter of Bethuel, who is a son of Milcah, the wife of Abraham's brother Nahor. She is therefore a grandniece of Abraham. As she fills her jug, the servant runs to her and asks for a sip of water. After she has given him a drink, she offers to draw water for the servant's camels. We have already been told that the girl was very beautiful, a virgin, untouched by man. So much has gone well thus far that the servant "watched her the whole time, silently waiting to learn whether or not the Lord had made his errand successful." When the camels had been watered, the servant produced gifts for Rebecca: a gold ring and two gold bracelets. Then he asked her: "Whose daughter are you?" "I am the daughter of Bethuel," she answers, "the son of Milcah whom she bore to Nahor." She invites the servant to stay at her home, assuring him that there is plenty of straw and fodder, and ample room.

> The man then bowed down in worship to the Lord, saying: "Blessed be the Lord, the God of my master Abraham, who has not let his constant kindness toward my master fail. As for myself also, the Lord has led me straight to the house of my master's brother."
>
> (Genesis 24:26-27)

We now meet, for the first time, the brother of Rebecca, Laban:

> As soon as he saw the ring and the bracelets on his sister Rebecca and heard her words about what the man had said to her, Laban rushed outside to the man at the spring.... He said to him: "Come, blessed of the Lord! Why are you staying outside when I have made the house ready for you, as well as a place for the camels?"
>
> (Genesis 24:30-31)

9

Further on in Genesis we will have a lot of opportunity to gauge the character of Laban, but here already we can easily gain the impression that Laban was much impressed by the gifts he beheld and by the camels (precious animals in desert country), and that he was more than anxious to have the servant stay with the family. Furthermore, the servant had identified himself as a servant of Abraham, and both Rebecca and Laban would therefore have known that he represented close kin.

These considerations, however, are not the essential items in the "saga" being enacted. If we have felt that the servant arrived at the gates of Abraham's kin all too quickly, with little or nothing said along the way, all of that changes now as the servant details graphically for his hearers (the family of Rebecca) the events that prompted his journey. Nothing seems to be left unsaid: every detail pertinent to the quest for a wife for Isaac must be set forth. Repetition is not intended to be tiresome: it emphasizes the goodness of Abraham's God in bringing the servant precisely to the solution for which he had prayed.

> "I am Abraham's servant," he began. "The Lord has blessed my master so abundantly that he has become a wealthy man; he has given him flocks and herds, silver and gold, male and female slaves, and camels and asses. My master's wife Sarah bore a son to my master in her old age, and he has given him everything he owns. My master put me under oath, saying: 'You shall not procure a wife for my son among the Canaanites in whose land I live. Instead, you shall go to my father's house, to my own relatives, to get a wife for my son.'"
>
> (Genesis 24:34-38)

The servant goes on to retell his own objections: "What if the woman will not follow me?" "The Lord, in whose presence I have always walked," Abraham had replied, "will send his messenger with you and make your errand successful, and so you will get a wife for my son from my own kindred of my father's house."

No ordinary story, you will say. Recall Paul's words as he wrote to the Romans: "Abraham believed God, and it was credited to him unto justice." That belief, that faith rings through the servant's explanation, and those listening to him readily understand that the events of which they are there and then a part are not chance circumstances, but a part of the mystery of God himself.

More of the details now follow, with the servant explaining his prayer uttered in the evening upon his arrival at the city in which his hearers live. The servant makes no attempt to summarize: the events he is recounting are far too important for that! Each detail of his prayer, each of the events that followed upon his prayer — Rebecca's coming out to draw water, her offer to give him a drink and to water his camels as well, her reply to his question about whose daughter she was, his presenting to her some of the jewelry that Abraham had given him — all of this must be told very carefully so that his hearers will understand something of the great mystery in which he and they are involved.

Are we so perceptive in the events of our lives? Do we see the hand of God operative in people we meet, tasks in which we are employed, the matter of our origins, our having been brought to the waters of baptism, our education in Christian discipleship? How easy, all too easy, to see life as humdrum, utterly bereft of mystery.

When the servant concluded his account, he asked that those listening to him let him know whether or not they are prepared to "show true love and loyalty to my master." Laban and his household said in reply:

> "This thing comes from the Lord; we can say nothing to you either for or against it. Here is Rebecca, ready for you; take her with you, that she may become the wife of your master's son, as the Lord has said."
>
> (Genesis 24:50-51)

We cannot help noticing the final words, "as the Lord has said." The sacred writer would have us see that all present recognized the mystery of which they were a part: not just Abraham said it, not just the servant said it. No, "as the Lord has said." There is a further bestowal of gifts on Rebecca, and the servant gave costly gifts also to her brother and mother. "After he (the servant) and the men with him had eaten and drunk, they spent the night there."

The very next day the servant wished to return to his master with Rebecca, but her mother and her brother wanted him to remain a short while, "stay ten days." But the servant pleaded his case, now that the Lord had made his journey successful. The issue is finally left to Rebecca: "Do you wish to go with this man?" they asked her. She answered: "I do."

Rebecca and her maids started out; they mounted the camels and followed the man. "So the servant took Rebecca and went on his way."

Upon his return to Canaan, the servant recounted to Isaac all the things he had done. "Then Isaac took Rebecca into his tent; he married her, and thus she became his wife. In his love for her Isaac found solace after the death of his mother Sarah" (Genesis 24:66-67).

Life is indeed a journey. Will it be taken with the Lord?

3

HE LAUGHS

Surely one of the most suspense-filled stories in the Book of Genesis concerns the conception and birth of the son of promise, Isaac. The Lord God would have none of the solutions to the problem proposed by those most involved: "One of my servants will be my heir," suggested Abram, and God took him outdoors to behold the stars in the sky. "Just so shall your descendants be," said the Lord. Sarai, also puzzled as to how God would accomplish offspring for her and her husband, suggested to Abram: "Have intercourse with my maid; perhaps I shall have sons through her." But that, too, turned out differently from what God had intended for Sarai. When, at a later date, three visitors appeared to Abraham (his name and that of Sarai had by now been changed) by the terebinth of Mamre, one of them said, "I will surely return to you about this time next year, and Sarah will then have a son." When Sarah finally conceived and bore Abraham a son in his old age, the boy was named Isaac (yitzak), "He laughs."

On the day of the boy's weaning, Abraham held a great feast, and when Sarah saw Ishmael, the son of her Egyptian maid, Hagar, playing with Isaac, she demanded of Abraham that he drive out the slave and her son. "No son of that slave," she asserted, "is going to share the inheritance of my son Isaac!" (Genesis 21:10). Already, in a sense, Isaac is being "acted upon," which is to say, that from this very early indication of someone else taking his part, protecting him, as it were, a pattern will begin to develop which clearly distinguishes Isaac from the three other major patriarchs of Genesis: Abraham, Jacob and Joseph.

The story of Abraham being told by God to sacrifice Isaac is well known, but what is not always so much thought about is the all but passive role of the boy. He raises only one question on the way to the land of Moriah where the sacrifice is to be offered: "Father, here are the fire and the wood, but where is the sheep for the holocaust?" (Genesis 22:7). The scriptural passage recounts nothing more from the boy, not even when Abraham bound him and placed him on top of the wood on the altar. It is an angel who intervenes, protecting the boy and instructing Abraham not to lay his hand upon him. Abraham spied a ram in the thicket and offered it up as a holocaust in place of his son. "Abraham named the site Yahweh-yireh; hence people now say, 'On the mountain the Lord will see'" (Genesis 22:14).

When Abraham had grown old he bade a trusted servant travel to Abraham's own land to find a wife for Isaac. The woman chosen, Rebecca, is portrayed in Genesis as a woman of action, of decision. When the betrothal is being effected by the servant of Abraham and a question arises as to how much time should elapse before the newly chosen bride should accompany the servant back to Canaan, the family opt for a delay of perhaps ten days. But when the question is placed before Rebecca, "Do you wish to go with this man?", she answers simply and unequivocally, "I do." At the conclusion of the return journey the servant related to Isaac all the things he had done. "Then Isaac took Rebecca into his tent; he married her, and thus she became his wife. In his love for her Isaac found solace after the death of his mother Sarah" (Genesis 24:67).

One hardly expects a grown man to have his wife chosen for him in the fashion narrated by Genesis; but all that transpires seems to accord perfectly with the portrait of Isaac shown forth by the sacred writer. Isaac was forty years old when he married Rebecca, and he entreated the Lord on behalf of his wife, since she was sterile. "The Lord heard his entreaty, and Rebecca became pregnant.... When the time of her delivery came, there were twins in her womb" (Genesis 25:21, 24). The firstborn, Esau, became a skillful hunter, and Isaac preferred him because he was fond of game. Rebecca, however, preferred Jacob.

The extraordinary blessings that the Lord had accorded to Abraham are reiterated for Isaac in the twenty-sixth chapter of Genesis, when, because of famine conditions in Canaan, Isaac travels to Gerar, in Philistine territory.

> Do not go down to Egypt, but continue to camp wherever in this land I tell you. Stay in this land, and I will be with you and bless you; for to you and your descendants I will give all these lands, in fulfillment of the oath that I swore to your father Abraham. I will make your descendants as numerous as the stars in the sky and give them all these lands, and in your descendants all the nations of the earth shall find blessing. (Genesis 26:3-4)

Isaac settled in Gerar, and when the men of the place inquired about his wife, he answered, "She is my sister." As with Abraham and Sarah on an earlier occasion, this led to difficulties with Abimelech, the king of Gerar, who at once gave orders to all his men: "Anyone who molests this man or his wife shall forthwith be put to death." Isaac became rich in Gerar, but because of water difficulties left and made the Wadi Gerar his campsite. Later he went up to Beer-sheba, and there the Lord appeared to him and said:

> I am the God of your father Abraham. You have no need to fear, since I am with you. I will bless you and multiply your descendants for the sake of my servant Abraham. (Genesis 26:24)

In some ways, the Gerar experience of Isaac, as recounted in Sacred Scripture, is the most assertive period of his life. Heretofore he seems to have been "acted upon," and the same will be true as he grows older and wishes to confer the blessing of the firstborn on his favored son, Esau. Rebecca prompts Jacob to grasp the blessing for himself. After Jacob has done so and is threatened with death by his brother Esau, Rebecca again takes matters into her own hands and tells Jacob to flee to her brother Laban, in Haran. Lest it seem to be her idea, she expresses to Isaac her disgust with the Hittite women whom Esau has married. Isaac thereupon calls Jacob and says:

> You shall not marry a Canaanite woman! Go now to Paddan-aram, to the home of your mother's father Bethuel, and there choose a wife for yourself from among the daughters of your uncle Laban. May God Almighty bless you and make you fertile, multiply you that you may become an assembly of peoples. May he extend to you and your descendants the blessing he gave to Abraham, so that you may gain possession of the land where you are staying, which he assigned to Abraham. (Genesis 28:1-4)

We do not hear of Isaac again until Jacob has returned from
Haran some twenty years later. On that occasion a reconciliation
is effected between Esau and Jacob. The final sentences on Isaac
read as follows: "The lifetime of Isaac was one hundred and eight
years; then he breathed his last. After a full life, he died as an old
man and was taken to his kinsmen. His sons Esau and Jacob buried him" (Genesis 35:28-29).

When we review the several chapters in which Isaac is spoken of, certain conclusions emerge. First, few sons are anticipated
with greater expectation and few seem to have so much depend-
ing on them if God's promise is to be fulfilled. All along the line
Isaac is prominent, yet seems far less an initiator of the action
around him than might have been expected. Almost from the
moment of his marriage forward, his wife exercises great resolve
and strength in carrying out plans. Isaac, it would seem, accepted
this. It is only in Gerar that Isaac himself appears to be planning
affairs. Even in the matter of the final blessing of the firstborn, Esau,
Isaac seems not to be angry: perturbed, certainly, but not angry.
Nevertheless, through Isaac the blessing originally imparted to his
father Abraham flows; Sacred Scripture never leaves us with a
modicum of doubt about that.

Is not Isaac the image of a person called to greatness, who
wishes that greatness to use him as it will? Whereas Abraham and
Jacob and Joseph are aggressive in the pursuit of their ends, Isaac
permits his life to be spent as God wills it, allowing those about
him to exercise whatever ingenuity they will to accomplish their
ends. To say this may seem to exaggerate and to place on Isaac's
shoulders a pattern of life to which he might not have deliberately
subscribed. In the long run, however, God's purposes are accomplished: the blessing extended to Abraham travels on through the

son of promise, Isaac, and through the latter to Jacob, who in turn becomes the father of the twelve tribes.

It is not simply Isaac that the reader wants to see in the Isaac cycle. Countless people are born into each day's life who are the bearers of myriad blessings that emerge without the slightest sign of aggressiveness. These, too, are God's children, and perhaps in our own lives we see similar patterns from time to time. Not every day is a major athletic contest or an important financial transaction in which extraordinary strength alone wins the day. The God of Abraham, Isaac and Jacob and Jesus continues to interest himself in the affairs of humanity, and is surely aware of the varied dispositions toward life that characterize all of us made in God's image and likeness. There is something important about Isaac's name: perhaps those who are willing to allow God's action in their lives to take them where God will, can, in the long run, count themselves among those who, Isaac-like, inwardly chuckle: "He laughs!"

4

LORD WE HAVE SINNED

e can hardly imagine a greater contrast than that experienced by the reader of Sacred Scriptures who moves from the final page of the Book of Genesis to the opening page of the Book of Exodus. As Genesis closes, all seems in good order: the patriarch Jacob has died and has been given appropriate funeral rites; whatever fear the brothers of Joseph had had that the latter would now take revenge has been laid to rest. Now Joseph himself had died and had been embalmed and laid to rest in a coffin in Egypt. One can foresee at that juncture nothing but good days ahead for the descendants of Jacob and their families.

The opening of the Book of Exodus reveals a very different kind of picture. "A new king, who knew nothing of Joseph, came to power in Egypt" (Exodus 1:8). Fearing the burgeoning population developing from Jacob's descendants, he began progressively to persecute the sons of Israel. The reader's first question might well be: Why this sudden change? The reality, of course, is that the change is not so sudden as the first page of Exodus might indicate, for some four hundred years elapse between the close of Genesis and the opening of Exodus. Not often, in reading a book, does one experience the lapse of four hundred years in turning a single page!

In his *Dictionary of the Bible*, Father John McKenzie writes:

> It appears that Asiatic groups began to invade Egypt about 1720 B.C. and continued to come in several waves for some years. In the anarchy which followed, the 12th Egyptian dynasty could offer no effective resistance.
>
> (page 380)

The invaders became known as Hyksos, sometimes referred to as nomad chieftains or shepherd kings. Egyptologists speak of them as "rulers of foreign lands." The Hyksos period is the most likely background for the story of Joseph and his brothers, and could help explain the royal favor that the descendants of Jacob received in Egypt. Following the close of Genesis, however, the Hyksos dynasty seems to have been overthrown when a stronger Egyptian dynasty recaptured the throne. Not unnaturally, Egyptian pharaohs were fearful of what might happen to their country if an enemy attacked and the sons of Jacob sided with the enemy. The very first chapter of Exodus tells us the sentiment of the Egyptians: "Come, let us deal shrewdly with them to stop their increase; otherwise, in time of war they too may join our enemies to fight against us" (Exodus 1:10). A systematic effort began on the part of the pharaoh to rid Israel of its male infants. Addressing himself to women who assisted in childbirth, the pharaoh instructed them: "When you act as midwives for the Hebrew women and see them giving birth, if it is a boy, kill him; but if it is a girl, she may live" (Exodus 1:16).

Into these unfavorable conditions the child Moses was born of levitical parents. Placed by the edge of the Nile by his mother, he is rescued by a daughter of the pharaoh and grows up in the court. As a young man he discovers a fellow Hebrew abused by an Egyptian, whom he kills. The spread of the word forces him to flee to Midian, where he marries a girl named Zipporah, daughter of Reuel. It is in Midian that he experiences a vision of a burning bush that is not consumed, and it is during this vision that he is directed by God to return to Egypt, to lead forth his people to freedom.

The obduracy of the pharaoh and the plagues used by God to set his people free are well known stories that lead ultimately to the first of two great highlights in the Book of Exodus, the crossing of the Sea of Reeds, placing Israel outside the grasp of the pharaoh. The second highlight will come with the Sinai experience, when Moses will be given the two tablets of the Law, on which are inscribed the Ten Words, most frequently spoken of as the Ten Commandments. A series of events between these great highlights or pilasters, as it were, is worthy of attention, before moving on to further aspects of the story of Israel's final victory.

Having escaped from Egypt (following the tenth plague, the death of the firstborn of the Egyptians), the children of Israel had not long been in the wilderness before serious problems began to arise. At Marah, for example, water was found that was too bitter to drink. The Lord instructed Moses to throw into the water a certain piece of wood, after which the water became fresh. Coming to Elim, where there were springs of water and palm trees, was a welcome relief; yet it was not long before complaints began about a lack of food. The Lord foretold that there would be bread from heaven and meat to eat, and both quail and manna were soon in evidence. When water again became a problem — more correctly, a lack of water — Moses was told to strike a rock at a place called Massah and Meriba, and water was provided by the Lord from the rock.

We cannot help seeing the extraordinary providence shown forth by God in behalf of his people over and over again. Students reading the Book of Exodus, in fact, sometimes raise a query: "Why is the Lord so good to this people when all they seem to do is to complain?" While the question is understandable, it reveals at the same time, perhaps, our own unconsciousness of attitudes now and then that are surely less than laudable. How easy for us to praise God and to believe that he really loves us as long as all is going well. But how suddenly the situation changes when we meet reverses, when things do not go our way. The remarkable thing that comes home to us in reading Exodus is the willingness of a people to reveal its own waywardness, its own limitations. So often we like people who read about us to see our virtues, our "good side"; seldom do we really want others to see our less attractive side. But this is precisely what the writers of Exodus have done: they have portrayed a people on the move, a people on pilgrimage, whose seamier characteristics are set forth as part and parcel of the journey.

Who is a greater hero than Moses? Yet even here the sacred text never hesitates to point up shortcomings. When Jethro (or Reuel), the father-in-law of Moses, comes to visit in the wilderness, he quickly perceives that Moses is endeavoring to accomplish the impossible in his efforts to judge the cases of all those who present themselves to Moses. Jethro points out to his son-in-law that the procedure he is following lacks sense: "What sort of thing is this that you are doing for the people? Why do you sit alone while all the people have to stand about you from morning till evening?" (Exodus 18:14). When Moses replies that all the people come to see him to have him consult God, to have a disagreement settled, Jethro is quite forthright: "You are not acting wisely; you will surely wear yourself out, and not only yourself but also these people with you. The task is too heavy for you; you cannot do it alone" (Exodus 18:17-18). Moses is then advised to look among the people for able and God-fearing men and to set them as officers over groups of thousands, of hundreds, of fifties, and of tens. They, in turn, can refer more important cases to Moses. The reply of Moses is at once simple and unaffected: he followed the advice of his father-in-law and did all that was suggested.

What comes through to us time and again in the Book of Exodus is a certain humility, a certain readiness to acknowledge guilt. At first sight, this may not seem so obvious: the sheer ingratitude of a people delivered from bondage may seem to loom over everything; but underneath that is something deeper — a recognition that everyone must say with the psalmist, "Lord, we have sinned." When, in the Book of Numbers, the people again complain because of the sparseness of their diet and saraph serpents appear among them, causing sickness and even death, "the people came to Moses and said, 'We have sinned in complaining against the Lord and you. Pray the Lord to take the serpents from us'" (Numbers 21:7). Moses is instructed by God to fashion a bronze serpent and to raise it as a standard. Anyone who was bitten and who now looked upon the bronze serpent would be healed. What we cannot help noting here again is that side by side with complaining was the inner awareness that such complaining hardly became a people rescued by God: repentance was much in order, and God's people knew it!

Early in the Gospel of Saint John we find a Pharisee named Nicodemus coming to Jesus at night and acknowledging that our Savior is from God, for "no one can do these signs that you are doing unless God is with him" (John 3:2). In the course of the conversation that ensues, Jesus makes reference to the serpent lifted up by Moses in the desert: "So must the Son of Man be lifted up, so that everyone who believes in him may have eternal life" (John 3:14-15). Prior to that our Savior had spoken of the necessity of being born from above if one is to see the kingdom of God. Christians early on came to see the bronze serpent of Numbers as a type of the crucified Jesus.

Is it not the appropriateness of repentance that the disciple of Jesus must ever bear in mind? Sight evanesces so easily when I forget about being born from above. Life can be seen as nothing more than coping with the everyday burdens that the marketplace imposes. But when life is undergirded, so to speak, by a recognition of our having been born from above, then the picture is altered markedly, and the Savior raised on the cross, like the serpent raised in the desert, can have cleansing power that helps us acknowledge our sinfulness in the presence of an all-holy God.

"Have mercy on me," cried out the psalmist, "have mercy on me, O God, in your goodness; in the greatness of your compassion wipe out my offense. Thoroughly wash me from my guilt and of my sin cleanse me" (Psalm 51:3-4). With our sisters and brothers who marched through the wilderness, let us, too, say, "Lord, we have sinned. Have mercy on us!"

5

I WILL SHOW YOU THE MAN YOU SEEK

I t sometimes happens in Sacred Scripture that an important event is narrated by the sacred writer and that following the recording of that event, a song or poem of praise and thanksgiving follows. Readers of the New Testament will recall perhaps the Canticle of Mary, sung by Our Lady when she visits Elizabeth, her kinswoman, and is saluted by Elizabeth in glowing terms. Prior to that visit Saint Luke had written of the annunciation to Zechariah, husband of Elizabeth, of John's conception, and of the announcement to Mary of her conception of Jesus. The time was appropriate, therefore, for a canticle of praise that now fell from the lips of Mary:

> My soul proclaims the greatness of the Lord;
> my spirit rejoices in God my savior.
> For he has looked upon his handmaid's lowliness;
> behold, from now on all ages will call me blessed.
> The Mighty One has done great things for me,
> and holy is his name.
> He has shown might with his arm,
> dispersed the arrogant of mind and heart.

He has thrown down the rulers from their thrones,
  but lifted up the lowly.
The hungry he has filled with good things;
  the rich he has sent away empty.
He has helped Israel his servant,
  remembering his mercy,
  according to his promise to our fathers,
  to Abraham and to his descendants forever.

(Luke 1:46-55)

In the Hebrew Scriptures, too, canticles of praise now and then follow upon extraordinary events. One thinks of the paean of praise rendered to God by Moses and the Israelites after the Chosen People had successfully crossed the Sea of Reeds and had beheld the pursuing Egyptians now overcome by those same waters.

I will sing to the Lord, for he is gloriously triumphant;
  horse and chariot he has cast into the sea.
My strength and my courage is the Lord,
  and he has been my savior.
He is my God, I praise him;
  the God of my father, I extol him.

(Exodus 15:1-2)

You may recall, too, the song of thanksgiving in the Book of Judith, a song led by Judith, the heroine of the story, and echoed by the people:

Strike up the instruments, a song to my God with timbrels,
  chant to the Lord with cymbals.
Sing to him a new song, exalt and acclaim his name.

(Judith 16:1)

The Book of Tobit, too, contains a song of praise, uttered in the light of the extraordinary mercies shown Tobit and his family:

> Blessed be God who lives forever,
>> because his kingdom lasts for all ages.
> For he scourges and then has mercy;
>> he casts down to the depths of the netherworld,
>> and he brings up from the great abyss.
>> (Tobit 13:1-2)

Early in the Second Book of Samuel the reader finds a threnody, sung by David upon hearing the tragic news of the death of Saul and his sons in their conflict with the Philistines:

> Alas! the glory of Israel,
>> Saul, slain upon your heights;
> How can the warriors have fallen!
>> Tell it not in Gath,
>> herald it not in the streets of Ashkelon,
> Lest the Philistine maidens rejoice,
>> lest the daughters of the strangers exult!
> Mountains of Gilboa,
>> may there be neither dew nor rain upon you,
>> nor upsurgings of the deeps!
> Upon you lie begrimed the warriors' shields,
>> the shield of Saul, no longer anointed with oil.
>> (2 Samuel 1:19-21)

The Book of Judges, which follows the Book of Joshua, continues in part the story of the settlement of the Promised Land. Judges were not court officials, but mostly military leaders, strong people who rose up now and then and led the Israelites during the many decades that preceded the inauguration of the monarchy. Following the judgeships of Othniel, Ehud and Shamgar, we come upon a prophetess, Deborah, who was judging Israel. "She used to sit under Deborah's palm tree, situated between Ramah and Bethel in the mountain region of Ephraim, and there the Israelites came up to her for judgment" (Judges 4:5). Summoning Barak, son of Abinoam, she told him that the Lord wanted him to gather an army to march against Sisera, general of Jabin's army.

Jabin was a Canaanite king into whose power Israel had fallen. Deborah promised Barak that she would lead Sisera out to the Wadi Kishon, together with his chariots and troops, and that she would there deliver Sisera into Barak's power.

> But Barak answered her: "If you come with me, I will go; if you do not come with me, I will not go." "I will certainly go with you," she replied, "but you shall not gain the glory in the expedition on which you are setting out, for the Lord will have Sisera fall into the power of a woman." (Judges 4:8-9)

Barak marched into battle, and before long the Lord put Sisera and his forces to rout. Sisera dismounted from his chariot and fled on foot. He came to the tent of Jael, wife of the Kenite Heber, who went out to meet him and said, "Come in, my lord, come in with me; do not be afraid."

> So he went into her tent, and she covered him with a rug. He said to her, "Please give me a little water to drink. I am thirsty." But she opened a jug of milk for him to drink and then covered him over. "Stand at the

entrance to the tent," he said to her. "If anyone comes and asks, 'Is there someone here?' say, 'No!'" Instead Jael, wife of Heber, got a tent peg and took a mallet in her hand. While Sisera was sound asleep, she stealthily approached him and drove the peg through his temple down to the ground, so that he perished in death.

(Judges 4:18-21)

While the poetic interpretation of a situation sometimes seems to resemble closely the prose account of the same incident or incidents, that is not always the case. The Song of Deborah is an excellent illustration of this. "The remarkable concluding section (Judges 5:24-31)," writes Robert Alter in *The Art of Biblical Poetry*, "which recounts the Canaanite general Sisera's death at the unflinching hands of Jael, is in itself an illuminating instance of the artistic possibilities of Hebrew verse narrative, and is all the more instructive because the way it shapes its materials can be handily compared with the prose version of the same events that precede the Song." (page 43)

The prose version, cited earlier, tells the reader that the events in Jael's tent ended in Sisera's death. The text then goes on to say that when Barak came in pursuit of the Canaanite general, Jael went out to meet him and said, "Come, I will show you the man you seek." So he went in with her, and there lay Sisera dead, with the tent peg through his temple (Judges 4:22). The poetic version to which Alter alludes above includes certain details of Sisera's death, but then goes on to offer the reader other considerations. The passage in question reads:

Blessed among women is Jael,
blessed among tent-dwelling women.

He asked for water, she gave him milk;
   in a princely bowl she offered curds.
With her left hand she reached for the peg,
   with her right, for the workman's mallet.
She hammered Sisera, crushed his head;
   she smashed, stove in his temple.
At her feet he sank down, fell, lay still;
   down at her feet he sank and fell;
   where he sank down, there he fell, slain.
From the window peered down and wailed
   the mother of Sisera, from the lattice:
"Why is his chariot so long in coming?
   why are the hoof beats of his chariots delayed?"
The wisest of her princesses answers her,
   and she, too, keeps answering herself;
"They must be dividing the spoil they took:
   there must be a damsel or two for each man.
Spoils of dyed cloth as Sisera's spoil,
   an ornate shawl or two for me in the spoil."
May all your enemies perish thus, O Lord!
   but your friends be as the sun
   rising in its might!   (Judges 5:24-31)

While the prose version has told the reader the bare facts concerning the death of Sisera, the more imaginative poetic version helps the reader appreciate the "atmosphere," so to speak, surrounding both the death itself and the people close to Sisera who could not but feel the impact of the general's death. One must note, too, the expansion — the poetic license, some might say — found even in describing Sisera's death: "She hammered Sisera," writes the poet, "crushed his head; she smashed, stove in his temple." And where the prose account noted simply the general's end — "so that he perished in death" — the poet offers a dramatic description of the general that intensifies with each telling: "At her feet he sank down, fell, lay still; down at her feet he sank and fell; where he sank down, there he fell, slain." The reader will not want to think that the poet wished simply to describe a gory end; rather, the triumph of Israel over its enemies is seen as the fulfillment of God's promise, a promise related to Barak by Deborah at the beginning of the story when she encouraged Israel's general to undertake the battle.

In every battle, in every war, there are both winners and losers, and often the victors have little time even to imagine the effect of enemy deaths on the families of the slain. The Canticle of Deborah deliberately imagines Sisera's mother wondering at the long delay in her son's return from battle. One of her princesses, in answering the mother's query, tries to console herself: she ruminates upon the division of spoil that inevitably follows upon a victory and the all-too-easily accepted practice of the military that allowed the soldiery to take for themselves one or another of the enemy's women. The poet does not dwell on the latter consideration, however, for in a moment the thought again is the spoil: what would Sisera bring home this time?

Over and again in the Hebrew Scriptures one finds triumphs that often give modern readers pause. It is important to remember that Israel often saw its wars as "holy battles," battles undertaken by God himself for the sake of his people. One need not endorse that kind of thinking, but the reader must try to see that that is often the prevailing attitude. How, then, does one trained in a Christian ethic look upon the historical events and their outcome?

Jael can be seen as a type of Mary, the Mother of God. Just as the reader of Genesis can relate the crushing of the serpent's head to the Mother of the Savior (graphically portrayed in some statues of the Immaculate Conception), and as in later books of the Hebrew Scriptures one sees Mary in the persons of Judith and Esther, so here may Jael be seen as a type, a figure of her whose life stood in opposition to evil and who, immaculately conceived, stood in everlasting contrariety to sin and its consequences.

Mary does not wield mallets or pick up tent pegs, but in a very different way she may be seen accomplishing in the history of redemption what Jael's victory achieved for the people of Israel: freedom from the deadliest of enemies.

6

ELECTED BY GOD

Sacred Scripture abounds with contrasts between persons, and often between persons who are closely related to each other. From almost the opening page we think of Cain and Abel. Once Abraham and Sarah are on the scene in the twelfth chapter of Genesis, there is the contrast between Ishmael, born of Hagar the slave girl, and Isaac, born of Abraham's true wife Sarah. In the very next generation we encounter Esau and Jacob, sons of Rebecca and Isaac.

A still greater contrast awaits us as the period of the monarchy gets underway. Saul is chosen as the first king of all Israel; after his death on Mount Gilboa, spoken of in the final chapter of the First Book of Samuel, David is chosen at first as king of his own tribe of Judah, but later is accepted by the other eleven tribes also, becoming therefore the second king of all Israel. When we contrast Saul and David, we find ourselves face to face with enormous differences.

A few years ago a monk of Saint Vincent Archabbey, Father Demetrius Dumm, wrote a book entitled *Flowers in the Desert*. In a chapter called "Our Response to God's Saving Event," he speaks at length of Saul and David, and we shall do well to quote here a sizeable paragraph from that chapter:

David was as self-confident and decisive as Saul was in-
secure and wavering. David had no liturgical scruples
when he and his men took and ate the sacred bread. David
also committed really serious sins, notably when he ordered the death of Uriah to cover up his sin with
Bathsheba. But he was able to repent and seemed to be
even better for the experience. Saul managed to turn
peccadilloes into unforgivable sins; David turned griev-
ous sins into opportunities for grace and growth.

(pages 41-42)

Long before the time of Saul's death, God had rejected him
from the possibility of an extended dynasty and had instructed the
prophet Samuel to seek a new king from the house of Jesse, in
Bethlehem, to replace Saul. Instructed by God, Samuel went to
Bethlehem, to the house of Jesse, and there asked to see Jesse's sons.
The first to appear was the eldest, Eliab. When Samuel saw him,
he thought: "Surely the Lord's anointed is here before him." But
the Lord said to Samuel: "Do not judge from his appearance or from
his lofty stature, because I have rejected him. Not as man sees does
God see, because man sees the appearance but the Lord looks into
the heart" (1 Samuel 16:6-7). The second son to appear was
Abinadab, but he was not chosen by the Lord either. Then came
Shammah, but Samuel said, "The Lord has not chosen this one
either." On through seven sons ran Jesse, only to discover that none
of them had been elected by God to be king. Almost in desperation Samuel cried out to Jesse: "Are these all the sons you have?"
Jesse replied: "There is still the youngest, who is tending the sheep."
Samuel insisted that he be called, and when he entered the Lord
said to Samuel, "There — anoint him, for this is he!"

Elected by God! Not the third son nor the fifth nor the seventh, but the youngest, David. Who knows the mind of God, or who can assay his ways? In our own lives, how can we gauge why God chose us, why we have been elected to stand in the ranks of the disciples of God's beloved Son? We are face to face with the greatest of mysteries of human life, the mystery of God's election.

One might be inclined to think that God had chosen David because David would be an unfailing servant. But David failed miserably, as Father Demetrius points out above, and not just once. Perhaps we think that because of being elected by God, David would not be subject to the hardships ordinarily experienced by his fellow humans; but that, too, proves contrary to David's history as it comes to the reader of the Books of Samuel and the early part of 1 Kings. David and his family would come to know incest, murder, treason — all kinds of vicissitudes that could easily conquer the spirit of a man. But through thick and thin David remains the Lord's elected, and "most of all, trusted God and life and himself enough to be able to do the risky, marginal things which are the hallmark of the truly free person" (Dumm, *op. cit.*, page 42).

What is the nature of David's life after he has been anointed by Samuel as the king to succeed Saul? Sacred Scripture gives the reader a picture that seems to indicate that the writer of the First Book of Samuel had more than one source with which to work and that the writer was not especially concerned about the chronological order of events. In the same chapter that recounts God's election of David, we read that the spirit of the Lord had departed from Saul and that the king was given to fits of melancholy. At the recommendation of his servants, Saul sent for a skillful harpist, David, to play for him and so soothe his troubled spirit.

"David came to Saul," writes the author of 1 Samuel, "and entered his service. Saul became very fond of him, and made him his armor-bearer, and sent Jesse the message, 'Allow David to remain in my service, for he meets with my approval'" (1 Samuel 16:21-22). In the following chapter, however, the reader comes upon the account of Goliath, the Philistine giant, challenging the Israelite army. David had come to visit his brothers, then serving as soldiers, and after hearing Goliath's threats, inquires of his brothers who this person is. David's brothers are annoyed with him, and in effect tell him to return to his sheep: war is a man's business! But David is not so easily put off, and word gets to Saul that David is willing to oppose Goliath. In what follows, the continuity of the story is such that one could guess that Saul had already met David, had known him as his skillful harpist, and so on. David tries on Saul's armor, finds it too cumbersome, and goes off armed with only sling and stones with which he overcomes the great Philistine. At the conclusion of the account the reader might easily wonder what has happened to the story line:

> When Saul saw David go out to meet the Philistine, he asked his general Abner, "Abner, whose son is that youth?" Abner replied, "As truly as your majesty is alive, I have no idea." And the king said, "Find out whose son the lad is." So when David returned from slaying the Philistine, Abner took him and presented him to Saul. David was still holding the Philistine's head. Saul then asked him, "Whose son are you, young man?" David replied, "I am the son of your servant Jesse of Bethlehem."   (1 Samuel 17:55-58)

Jonathan, the son of Saul, becomes friendly with David, and when, following the victory over Goliath, women begin to sing in the streets, "Saul has slain his thousands and David his ten thousands," Saul becomes intensely jealous of David, thinking that nothing remains for the young man except the throne itself. Later David marries the younger daughter of Saul, Michal, really a plot on the part of Saul to ensnare David, though Michal is said to be deeply in love with David.

The remainder of the First Book of Samuel is an account of Saul's pursuit of David, of the king's effort to trap David in one way or another. On two separate occasions David has a perfect opportunity to take Saul's life. On the first of these occasions David and his followers are hidden in the inner recesses of a cave which Saul enters to relieve nature. David's followers encouraged him to take advantage of the opportunity to end the king's life, but David would not lift a finger against the Lord's anointed. The second occasion arises when David and a companion enter the tent of Saul by night, only to find the king and his general, Abner, sound asleep. Again David was in a perfect position to slay the king, but for a second time he refused to allow that the Lord's anointed be touched.

At the very end of the First Book of Samuel, Saul is pitted against the Philistines on Mount Gilboa and is wounded. When Saul's armor-bearer refuses to end the king's life, though Saul had asked him to do so, the king falls on his own sword and dies. With him have died several of his sons, including David's dear friend, Jonathan. When word is brought to David concerning the outcome of the battle, clearly a victory for the Philistines, David chants an elegy for Saul and Jonathan in testimony of his genuine sorrow: "How can the warriors have fallen, the weapons of war have perished!" (2 Samuel 1:27)

David is eventually chosen as king by all of Israel's twelve tribes, and the Second Book of Samuel conveys to the reader an account of David's reign. As indicated earlier, the account is not completely a story of glory, yet throughout the story David remains the elect of God. One of the early Fathers of the Church, commenting on the less glorious aspects of David's kingship, writes:

"David sinned, and that is common for kings; David repented, and that is not so common for kings." The reader of Sacred Scripture sees in David's sinfulness in the case of Bathsheba and Uriah, not simply the temporary downfall of a truly great king; rather, the reader will recognize that sin all too often accompanies the elect of God, including oneself. But God's mercy does not then and there depart from the king. Punishment does indeed come his way in the several catastrophes narrated concerning the king's own family. David recognizes those evils as the consequence of his own sinfulness, and throughout the remainder of his life he remains faithful to the God who elected him for his own.

When the court prophet Nathan comes to David, following the death of Uriah, he tells a parable that has become familiar through the centuries, a parable about a wealthy man who had many flocks depriving a poor man who had but one ewe lamb, in order to entertain the rich man's guest. "The man who has done this merits death!" cried David. Nathan, in reply, says to the king, "You are the man!" This tiny sentence has come down to us through the years, reminding each of us that we are ourselves often guilty of the very things in which we stand in judgment on others. But we ought not stop there: the king quickly responds to Nathan, "I have sinned against the Lord."

Each of us has been elected by the God in whose image and likeness we have been created. Yet we, too, like the great David, have sinned against the Lord. To have sinned does not mean to have lost our election by God; indeed, although we have sinned a thousand times over, we are called back time and again to an awareness of the greatness that is ours because of our election. Why? So that the destiny that is ours may be achieved in the end — everlasting happiness in the kingdom that the Lord Jesus came to establish.

7

YOU ARE THE MAN

Perhaps one of the most poignant scenes in the Hebrew Scriptures is found in the early part of the Second Book of Samuel. David has been chosen by his own tribe of Judah to rule as king, but the other tribes had chosen the only remaining son of Saul, Ishbaal, to rule as their king. Ishbaal's general, Abner, is accused by the king of familiarity with a concubine of Saul, Rizpah, and Abner takes umbrage at this, threatening to undermine the kingdom of Ishbaal and to deliver its loyalties to David.

When Abner later sends word to David of his desire to meet with him, David responds that he is open to some kind of agreement, but insists that Abner not come to him unless he is accompanied by Michal, daughter of the deceased Saul and David's former wife. At the same time, David sends messengers to Ishbaal, saying, "Give me my wife Michal, whom I espoused by paying a hundred Philistine foreskins" (2 Samuel 3:14).

> Ishbaal sent for her and took her away from her husband Paltiel, son of Laish, who followed her weeping as far as Bahurim. But Abner said to him, "Go back!" And he turned back.   (2 Samuel 3:15-16)

When we speak of social justice, we want to think not simply in terms of overall conditions of a given set of people, but of the individual person especially. Paltiel, husband of Michal, is seen here as a victim of kingly power: who could resist King David of Judah, or who could resist Abner, general of Ishbaal's army? We see here sheer power at work, the power of the establishment, if you will, over against the powerlessness of a man who apparently dearly loved his wife.

When the prophet Amos was bidden by God, in the course of the eighth century B.C.E., to leave his native Tekoa and to go north to the city of Bethel, where King Jeroboam II and his court lived and worshiped, Amos prophesied in terms of the injustice found there:

> Thus says the Lord:
> For three crimes of Israel, and for four,
>   I will not revoke my word;
> Because they sell the just man for silver,
>   and the poor man for a pair of sandals,
> They trample the heads of the weak
>   into the dust of the earth,
>   and force the lowly out of the way.
> Son and father go to the same prostitute,
>   profaning my holy name.
> Upon garments taken in pledge
>   they recline beside my altar;
> And the wine of those who have been fined
>   they drink in the house of their god.   (Amos 2:6-8)

There is no misreading the prophet: the crimes he cites clearly violate the claims of justice that are well known to God's people. Micah, a contemporary of Amos, writes in similar vein:

Woe to those who plan iniquity,
    and work out evil on their couches;
In the morning light they accomplish it
    when it lies within their power.
They covet fields, and seize them;
    houses, and they take them;
They cheat an owner of his house,
    a man of his inheritance.
Therefore, thus says the Lord:
Behold, I am planning against this race an evil
    from which you shall not withdraw your necks;
Nor shall you walk with head high,
    for it will be a time of evil.   (Micah 2:1-3)

Later in his prophecy Micah writes:

You have been told, O man, what is good,
    and what the Lord requires of you:
Only to do the right and to love goodness,
    and to walk humbly with your God.   (Micah 6:8)

What Amos says of Israel, Micah says of Judah: God's people are hardly his people in the injustices they demonstrate toward those around them. Micah makes abundantly clear what God is asking: to do the right and to love goodness.

In the First Book of Kings the prophet Elijah finds himself called by God to remonstrate with King Ahab for his criminal action respecting a man who owned a vineyard next to the king's palace. From the prophet's first appearance in Israel, a kind of contest had ensued between prophet and king because of Ahab's encouragement of syncretism: Jahweh was indeed acknowledged as

Israel's God, yet Baal worship was evident on every side. The wife of the king, Queen Jezebel, had brought with her to Israel, when she married Ahab, not only her preference for Baal worship, but also a host of Baal prophets. But in the matter now under discussion it is not the obvious syncretism in worship against which Elijah is protesting, but rank injustice toward a fellow human being, simply because the latter held a piece of ancestral property adjacent to the king's that Ahab very much wanted.

When Ahab approached Naboth to ask for the vineyard next to his own, he offered in exchange another piece of property. Should Naboth not be interested in an alternate piece of property, said the king, Ahab would be happy to give Naboth money. The reaction of Naboth may have surprised the king: "The Lord forbid," Naboth answered the king, "that I should give you my ancestral heritage." Levitical law provided for the non-alienation of patrimony, and surely the king realized this: were it not for that, he might somehow have forced Naboth to relinquish the property in question. "Ahab went home disturbed and angry at the answer Naboth the Jezreelite had made to him" (1 Kings 21:4). Like a petulant child, he took to his bed and refused to eat.

Whatever the failings of Queen Jezebel, she knew her husband well and recognized at once the kind of reversal he had encountered. When Ahab's explanation assured her that it was simply a matter of a piece of ancestral property, she assured the king that she would take care of matters promptly. And take care she did, in one of Sacred Scripture's most forceful examples of rank injustice done to a person powerless to protect himself. She sent word, under the king's seal, to the elders and nobles who lived in the same city with Naboth, ordering them to proclaim a fast and to set Naboth at the head of the people. Next, she instructed them to get two scoundrels to face him and to accuse him of having cursed God and king. "Then take him out and stone him to death" (1 Kings 21:10).

> His fellow citizens — the elders and the nobles who dwelt in his city — did as Jezebel had ordered them in writing, through the letters she had sent them. They proclaimed a fast and placed Naboth at the head of the people. Two scoundrels came in and confronted him with the accusation, "Naboth has cursed God and king." And they led him out of the city and stoned him to death. Then they sent the information to Jezebel that Naboth had been stoned to death. (1 Kings 21:11-14)

Our first inclination, upon reading this kind of tale, is perhaps one of great revulsion: what wickedness, we may say to ourselves, what gross injustice! But Sacred Scripture, we want to remember, is ever present to challenge us, to ask whether our lives accord with such unprincipled conduct, or whether we are making valiant efforts to render to our neighbor whatever is her or his due. The prophetic voice needs to be present to us, holding up the mirror of Scripture to us, to see what kind of reflection is forthcoming.

Once Jezebel received word of Naboth's stoning, she said to Ahab, "Go on, take possession of the vineyard of Naboth the Jezreelite which he refused to sell you, because Naboth is not alive, but dead." The king started off at once to take possession of the coveted vineyard. But the prophetic voice, not from within but from without, was waiting: the Lord bade Elijah meet Ahab en route to the vineyard.

This is what you shall tell him. "The Lord says: 'After murdering, do you also take possession?' For this, the Lord says: 'In the place where the dogs licked up the blood of Naboth, the dogs shall lick up your blood, too.'"

(1 Kings 21:19)

When Elijah met the king, he delivered God's message, and added that a similar fate would befall Jezebel also.

In an earlier period of Israel's history, King David sat on the throne, governing both Israel and Judah. On one occasion, while his army was away, battling the Ammonites, David rose from his siesta

and strode about the roof of the palace. From the roof he saw a woman bathing, who was very beautiful. David had inquiries made about the woman and was told, "She is Bathsheba, daughter of Eliam, and wife of Joab's armor-bearer, Uriah the Hittite." Then David sent messengers and took her. When she came to him, he had relations with her.... She then returned to her house. But the woman had conceived, and sent the information to David, "I am with child." (2 Samuel 11:2-5)

David then sent for Uriah, welcomed him heartily, and bade him be at ease: "Go down to your house and bathe your feet." Uriah, however, refused to go down to his house, contending that as long as his fellow-soldiers were in the field, he could hardly enjoy the comfort of his home. Despite David's getting Uriah drunk, the soldier remained steadfast in his resolution. Finally, in sheer desperation, David sent Uriah back to the army, despatching with him a message for Joab, general of David's army. Contained in the message were instructions to see to it that in the next engagement, Uriah was to be placed in front, where the fighting would be fierce. Joab obliged the king, and Uriah was killed.

We must pause here to consider the crassness of David. Not only does he mastermind a plan to cover over his adultery. Not only has he kept egging Uriah on to enjoy the comfort of his household. Not only does he now send Uriah back to the army. In addition to all these things, he entrusts to Uriah a message for Joab which contains instructions for Uriah's demise. Justice? Care for one's fellow-being? Passion and fear of disgrace had eliminated these considerations, prompting the king to act shamelessly and grievously.

Fortunately, the voice of the prophet was at hand: the court prophet Nathan approaches the king and relates to him a parable about a rich man who, entertaining a guest, took the only ewe lamb of a poor man to serve dinner for the guest. David, overcome with wrath, exclaims: "As the Lord lives, the man who has done this merits death! He shall restore the ewe lamb fourfold because he has done this and has had no pity" (2 Samuel 12:5). It did not take Nathan long to make his reply to the king: "You are the man!"

As each of us examines self to consider our concern or lack of it in matters of justice, the words of Nathan may tend to ring out: "You are the woman! You are the man!" Fortunately, our God is merciful and listens to our pleas for mercy and is ready to forgive. May the Scriptures nevertheless remind us over and again that we, too, are to be filled with mercy, conscious always of the dictum bequeathed to us in the Gospel by the Lord Jesus: "Whatever you do to one of these, my least brethren, you do also unto me."

8

THE MASTIC AND THE OAK

or the reader of the Book of Daniel, an engaging experience comes with the thirteenth chapter, in which is recounted the story of Susanna, wife of Joakim, a man of means whose extensive gardens were available to the townspeople nearby. Two elders, who were appointed judges, became enamored of Susanna, and each considered how he might obtain her favors. One day the two elders took leave of each other, both supposedly going home for the midday meal, when suddenly both found themselves in Joakim's gardens. Both then acknowledged their passion for Susanna and plotted together to obtain their end.

On a given day Susanna entered the gardens accompanied by two maids. Because it was warm she decided to bathe, and bade her maids obtain oil and soap. The elders, as soon as the maids had left, hurried to Susanna, spoke of their desire, and threatened Susanna that unless she acceded to their wishes, they would accuse her of lying with a young man, there in the bathing area. Although she felt herself trapped, Susanna said, "It is better for me to fall into your power without sin than to sin before the Lord" (Daniel 13:23). She shrieked, and the old men also shouted at her. "At the accusations by the old men, the servants felt very much ashamed, for never had any such thing been said about Susanna" (Daniel 13:27).

The two judges were fully determined to put Susanna to death, and a trial was arranged in which both testified that as they were walking in Joakim's gardens, a young man had come and had lain with Susanna. "The man we could not hold," they continued, "because he was stronger than we; he opened the doors and ran off" (Daniel 13:39). But Susanna cried aloud: "O eternal God, you know what is hidden and are aware of all things before they come to be: you know that they have testified falsely against me" (Daniel 13:42-43). The Lord heard her prayer, and as she was being led off to execution, God stirred up the holy spirit of a young boy named Daniel, and he cried aloud: "I will have no part in the death of this woman" (Daniel 13:45-46). When the people turned and asked him what he was saying, he replied: "Are you such fools, O Israelites! To condemn a woman of Israel without examination and without clear evidence? Return to court, for they have testified falsely against her" (Daniel 13:48-49).

The people returned in haste, and Daniel called for the two elders to be separated.

> After they were separated one from the other, he called one of them and said: "How you have grown evil with age! Now have your past sins come to term: passing unjust sentences, condemning the innocent, and freeing the guilty, although the Lord says, 'The innocent and the just you shall not put to death.' Now, then, if you were a witness, tell me under what tree you saw them together." "Under a mastic tree," he answered. "Your fine lie has cost you your head," said Daniel; "for the angel of God shall receive the sentence from him and split you in two." (Daniel 13:52-55)

We may at first wonder at Daniel's exclamation upon hearing that the elder reported seeing the couple under a mastic tree. In the Greek language there is a play on words here: "mastic tree" and "split" are closely related. For the first, the Greek reads *hypo schinon*, and for the second, *schisel*.

> Putting him to one side, he ordered the other one to be brought. "Offspring of Canaan, and not of Judah," Daniel said to him, "beauty has seduced you, lust has subverted your conscience. This is how you acted with the daughters of Israel, and in their fear they yielded to you; but a daughter of Judah did not tolerate your wickedness. Now then, tell me under what tree you surprised them together." "Under an oak," he said. "Your fine lie has cost you also your head," said Daniel, "for the angel of God waits with a sword to cut you in two so as to make an end of you both."   (Daniel 13:56-59)

Again there is a play on words in the Greek: this time the related words are "oak" and "cut." For "under an oak," the Greek would read *hypo prinon*, and for "cut" the Greek reads *prisal*.

The entire assembly rejoiced at what they had heard, and the unjust elders were put to death. "Thus was innocent blood spared that day," the account concludes. In a brief sentence or two the text tells the reader that everyone close to Susanna rejoiced and that Daniel, from that day forward, was greatly esteemed by the people.

When the Church recounts the story of Susanna in her liturgy (Monday of the Fifth Week of Lent), she accompanies it with a passage from the Gospel of Saint John, the story of the adulteress. There are many differences, of course, in the two stories, but there are also certain features that relate the two. In the case of Susanna, there has been no adultery, but rather the unjust charge of adultery by the conscienceless elders; in the Johannine account, the woman brought to Jesus is said to have been caught in adultery. The matter that relates the two accounts is the overwhelming desire of those accusing the woman in the story to have her put to death.

It was the hope of those who brought the woman to Jesus not only to effect the woman's death, but also to trap our Savior. Hence their question: "Now in the law, Moses commanded us to stone such women. What do you say?" (John 8:5). The adversaries of Jesus are in seemingly perfect position: should Jesus say that the woman ought not be stoned, he would be in clear violation of the Mosaic law; if, on the other hand, he assented to her stoning, he would not appear to be the kind and gentle Jesus portrayed throughout the Gospel. As Jesus writes on the ground with his finger, some would have the reader believe that our Savior is writing out the sins of the woman's accusers. The Gospel, however, does not suggest that. "But when they continued asking him, he straightened up and said to them, 'Let the one among you who is without sin be the first to throw a stone at her.' Again he bent down and wrote on the ground" (John 8:7-8).

We are at once aware that Jesus has neither said to stone the woman nor not to stone her; rather, he has called attention to the sins of those accusing the woman. Yet even that is not the high point, in a way, of the account. The accusers leave one by one, beginning with the elders, and our Savior is left alone with the accused. "Woman, where are they? Has no one condemned you?" We must contemplate those two questions: there were a thousand others that Jesus might have placed. But the two questions he asks can in no way embarrass the woman. She is able to respond that no one has condemned her. "Neither do I condemn you," said Jesus. "Go, and from now on do not sin any more."

The juxtaposition of the Daniel and John texts toward the latter part of the Lenten season can say much to each of us. The Susanna story reminds us of our own weaknesses, not least of all respecting the flesh. At the same time, the text tells us how very sinful it is to accuse innocent people. The case need not be as grave as was the situation with Susanna: even in lesser matters our discipleship keeps calling us to speak with honesty about our neighbor, and especially cautions us against accusing others of faults or sins of which they are not guilty.

The Johannine text is, in the first place, a call to mercy toward sinners. In no way does Jesus whitewash adultery; that is not the point of the story at all. But his actions (silence at first) and his words remind those present that no one is without sin. When we tend to be judgmental of others, John's eighth chapter can be a powerful and effective reminder of where we ought to stand: among the countless sinners who have experienced over and again in the course of a lifetime the ever-forgiving mercy of God. The questions, too, addressed by the Savior of mankind to the adulteress, are models for us: we can easily embarrass one another, or we can place questions that help the sinner find again that self-esteem without which life can be quite unbearable.

One final note may be added to the above by pointing up the appropriate responsory psalm chosen by the liturgy for the Susanna reading on Monday of the Fifth Week of Lent. "Even though I walk in the dark valley," reads the response, "I fear no evil; for you are at my side." Taken from a psalm familiar to everyone, Psalm 23, the response readily reminds us of the disposition that could well have been Susanna's in the face of the false accusations made against her. (It is not unthinkable, either, that the adulteress of John's

Gospel would have known much walking in a dark valley.) Despite the dark valley, Susanna recognized an all-holy God who sees truth and recognizes virtue; it was to that God that she had entrusted herself from the very moment in which she was challenged. The psalm is one that we can keep close to ourselves, in season and out of season, because for each of us there are now and then dark valleys, and it is good to remember that the Shepherd of us all is ever present, walking with us without fail.

9

IS THE ARM OF GOD SHORT?

One of the most devastating experiences in the history of the Chosen People came in the year 587 B.C.E., when the armies of King Nebuchadnezzar of Babylon besieged Jerusalem, destroyed much of the temple, pulled down the walls surrounding the city, and carted off to Babylon hundreds of the residents of Jerusalem, including King Zedekiah and his courtiers. Something of the pathos of the captivity, better known as the Exile, is reflected in Psalm 137: "By the waters of Babylon we sat and wept when we remembered Zion." Zion is the mountain or hill on which the temple was located, and the very thought of being exiled from Zion and from all it signified was a source of heartache for those forced to relinquish their homeland.

Hundreds of years earlier God had sent prophets to speak to his people, to encourage them in their observance of the covenant enacted at Mount Sinai under the great Moses, and to wean them away from the worship of Baal, a constant temptation to them almost from the moment they had set foot in the Land of Promise. Both Amos and Hosea had exercised their ministry of prophecy in the northern kingdom of Israel, exhorting, cajoling, threatening, but all to no avail. In the year 721 B.C.E., Samaria, the capital of

Israel, fell to the Assyrians, a strong power to the north and east, and great numbers of people were carried off, never to return.

Contemporaries of Amos and Hosea, the prophets Isaiah and Micah, and a bit later, Jeremiah, prophesied in the southern kingdom of Judah, and it was then no secret that Samaria had fallen. Exhortations in Judah, however, seemed to be of little use. When Jeremiah came to prophesy, the Lord God had become so impatient with Judah that he told Jeremiah to instruct his fellow Judahites not to resist the armies of Babylon when they came. Not unnaturally, this seemed to the courtiers of Judah a clear sign of a treasonous bent on the part of Jeremiah.

The Book of Lamentations, one of Scripture's most poignant books, gives us an insight into the conditions that prevailed in Jerusalem, God's chosen city, after Babylon's conquest:

> How lonely is she now, the once crowded city!
> Widowed is she who was mistress over nations;
> The princess among the provinces has been made a
> toiling slave. (Lamentations 1:1)

There is a consciousness in the sacred author that Jerusalem's fate has been brought upon herself: "The Lord has punished her for her many sins. Her little ones have gone away, captive before the foe." Conditions in the city are grave: "All her people groan, searching for bread." In a text that came, in New Testament times, to be applied to the Person of Jesus, the sacred writer unveils the bitterness of Jerusalem's situation:

> Come all you who pass by the way,
>   look and see
> Whether there is any suffering like my suffering,

which has been dealt me
When the Lord afflicted me
on the day of his blazing wrath.

(Lamentations 1:12)

If ever there was a time for the Chosen People to remember their history, surely it was now: not just the history of the immediate past, but of that long history that had found them in the wilderness centuries earlier under Moses, making their way ever so slowly to the Promised Land. When, in the Book of Numbers, God speaks to Moses about complaints he had heard from the people concerning food and drink, he tells Moses that he is well aware of the people's needs and that they will have meat not for one day or two days, or five, or ten or twenty days, but for a whole month. But Moses said, "The people around me include six hundred thousand soldiers; yet you say, 'I will give them meat to eat for a whole month'" (Numbers 11:19, 21). The Lord answered Moses, "Is the arm of God short?"

In Babylon, too, the people who had gone off into exile from Jerusalem were given ample opportunity to consider afresh God's great mercies of the past. Could not God do the same for his people now? If God had been able to provide meat and bread and water for the Chosen People during their long years in the desert, why could not God now again do something for his people? What was at first not realized was this, that God had permitted the triumph of Babylon over Judah and Jerusalem as a means by which to purify his people. If the voices of the prophets with their constant warnings had not been able to turn the people away from the Baals and the shallow religious practice that accompanied Baal worship, God would use Babylon to effect what the voice of the prophets had not been able to accomplish.

The shifting political fortunes of the major powers in the East could also be used by the Lord God to achieve his purposes for his people. The Chosen People had been in Babylon for perhaps half a century when a new king arose in Persia, Cyrus by name, who would in time become the instrument of Israel's deliverance. His stature came to exceed that of the Babylonians, and once Cyrus had overpowered Babylon a decree was issued that reversed the fortunes of God's people.

> Thus says Cyrus, king of Persia: "All the kingdoms of the earth the Lord, the God of heaven, has given to me, and he has also charged me to build him a house in Jerusalem, which is in Judah. Whoever, therefore, among you belongs to any part of his people, let him go up, and may his God be with him." (2 Chronicles 36:23)

Before long the consoling voice of Second Isaiah would be heard, speaking to his people: "Comfort, give comfort to my people, says your God. Speak tenderly to Jerusalem, and proclaim to her that her service is at an end, her guilt is expiated; indeed, she has received from the hand of the Lord double for all her sins" (Isaiah 40:1-2). This prophet of great empathy had suffered with his people in the Exile; but now he is able to read the signs of the times, and he recognizes that the Lord is about to accomplish a great act for his people, their return to Zion, to Jerusalem. He speaks of the Lord making straight the way, of filling in valleys, of making low the mountains and hills, of preparing a way for the Lord in the desert. For Second Isaiah, the return to Jerusalem will be a second Exodus, even greater than the first, manifesting the continued presence of God's mercy: God's arm is not short.

Often in our lives we discover that the reality we had anticipated seems much less than the expectation had been, and so it was with the exiles returning to Zion. The temple was a virtual shambles, the walls surrounding the city had been torn down for the most part, and the population of Jerusalem was relatively small. Where was the great homecoming that the returning exiles had anticipated? Again the Lord is at hand, raising prophetic voices to encourage the people and to draw their attention to specific needs.

> Thus says the Lord of hosts: "This people says: 'Not now has the time come to rebuild the house of the Lord.' Is it time for you to dwell in your own paneled houses, while this house lies in ruins?"   (Haggai 1:2, 4)

The prophet Zechariah, speaking at the same time as Haggai, also encourages the people: "Therefore says the Lord: I will turn to Jerusalem in mercy; my house shall be built in it, says the Lord of hosts, and a measuring line shall be stretched over Jerusalem" (Zechariah 1:16). Despite what may seem to be adverse circumstances, the people are to rebuild the Lord's temple.

How often in our own lives discouragement tempts us to forgo rebuilding: not a temple, not a church, not a house, but simply our own lives and the lives of those around us. "Unless the Lord build the house," sings the psalmist, "they labor in vain who build it. Unless the Lord guard the city, in vain does the guard keep vigil" (Psalm 127:1). It is always the Lord who has to build our house, it is the Lord who must keep vigil in our city; but if we lack confidence in the Lord, if we fail to trust him, how can the house be rebuilt? That, in effect, is precisely the message that Haggai and Zechariah endeavor to deliver to the returned exiles. However discouraging the situation, we are to trust the Lord, we are to help rebuild "his house."

For the people of Jerusalem, rebuilding the Lord's house was essential, for the temple signified the presence of Torah, of God's covenant with his people. Centuries earlier, recall, when David became king of the twelve tribes of Israel, his shrewdness told him that unity would never prevail among his people apart from their real center, the Lord God of heaven and earth. Small wonder that David, in transferring the Ark of the Covenant, the vessel that contained the Tablets of the Law, danced before the Ark as it approached Jerusalem, his newly chosen capital. At a later date, David's son Solomon would create a magnificent temple to house the Ark and to serve as a central place of worship for all God's people. Now, following the exile, it is again essential that the center be emphasized: the prophets raised up by God keep encouraging the people to build for the Lord. The Lord, in turn, will "build" for his people.

The psalmist has written: "I rejoiced because they said to me, 'We will go up to the house of the Lord.' And now we have set foot within your gates, O Jerusalem, Jerusalem, built as a city with compact unity" (Psalm 122:1). Note the thrill conveyed by the psalmist at the very thought of going up to Jerusalem.

That same kind of thrill wants to take hold of us as we set about the rebuilding process that is at times needed in each of our lives. With Haggai and Zechariah we are never to imagine that the arm of God is short.

10

ROAMING THE EARTH AND PATROLLING IT

No book in all of Sacred Scripture addresses itself more directly to the problem of evil than the Book of Job. Why do the innocent suffer? The question did not originate with Job, of course, but the difficulty of suffering, particularly human suffering (especially when that seems undeserved) comes clearly into focus as we listen to Job, his friends, and finally God, in the Book of Job.

In 587 B.C.E., you will recall, the Babylonian armies attacked Jerusalem and, after severely damaging the great temple of Solomon and pulling down the walls that surrounded the city, carried away hundreds of Jerusalemites into exile in Babylon. Today, centuries later, we are still moved by the psalmist's cry: "How could we sing a song of the Lord in a foreign land?" We feel, somehow, that we understand the exiles who found it all but impossible to sing a song of Zion there by the waters of Babylon. Was it from this bitter experience that the Book of Job came into being? Some believe so.

Job's story is well known: a good man of great estate becomes the subject of a wager between God and "the Satan," as some translators call him. In the first phase of the wager Satan bets that Job, deprived of his wealth, will blaspheme God. When that does not eventuate — "The Lord has given," says Job, "and the Lord has taken away; praised be the name of the Lord!" — Satan again appears before God, ready to try a second device. "Skin for skin!" It is only when a man's body begins to writhe in pain, suggests Satan, that he really wonders about the goodness and greatness of God. The second part of the wager is then entered upon, but Satan is not permitted to take Job's life.

At this juncture a series of dialogues gets underway between Job and three of his friends. Job speaks first, then Eliphaz, the first of the three friends; Job replies, and then the second friend, Bildad, takes up the discussion; again Job comments, and the third friend, Zophar, speaks. In all, there are three sets of dialogues, though the last set is incomplete. Throughout the conversations, Job steadfastly maintains his innocence, while the friends of Job believe that guilt must lurk somewhere, else God would not be trying Job so painfully. This is the nub of the debate, if one may so call it: Job knows that he is suffering bitterly but does not know why; the three friends of Job keep insisting that he must have done something, else God would not have afflicted him with such great distress. If we would penetrate the argument further, however, we need to hear the arguments advanced both by Job's friends and by the protagonist himself.

When Satan first appeared at the council of the Lord and was asked whence he came, he responded, "From roaming the earth and patrolling it." As one listens to the conversations of Job and his friends, it is good to remember that Satan continues to do just that — to roam the earth and to patrol it.

The first cycle of speeches begins with Job bewailing his birth: "Perish the day on which I was born" (Job 3:3). He continues in this vein and is answered by Eliphaz, who sounds just a bit annoyed as he remarks: "If someone attempts a word with you, will you mind? For how can anyone refrain from speaking?" (Job 4:2). He reminds Job that the latter has instructed many; but now, complains Eliphaz, Job is himself impatient. "Impatience kills the fool," continues Eliphaz, "and indignation slays the simpleton" (Job 5:2). When Job replies, he is by no means shaken by his friend's observations, for he continues to believe that his present condition is inexplicable. "Could my anguish but be measured," he retorts, "and my calamity laid with it in the scales, they would now outweigh the sands of the sea" (Job 6:2-3). "Teach me," he continues, "and I will be silent; prove to me wherein I have erred." For Job, man's life on earth is a drudgery, his days those of a hireling. The psalmist had written: "What is man that you should be mindful of him, or the son of man that you should care for him?" (Psalm 8:5). Job has a different twist: "What is man, that you make much of him, or pay him any heed?" (Job 7:17). Job's objection is that God observes man with each new day and tries him every moment! "Though I have sinned, what can I do to you, O watcher of men? Why do you not pardon my offense, or take away my guilt?" (Job 7:21). Even if Job's friends are correct in insisting that he has sinned (which Job is not really prepared to acknowledge), what difference does that really make to God, asks Job: why not take away my offense!

Job's second friend, Bildad, is also unmoved it would appear: "How long will you utter such things? The words from your mouth are like a mighty wind!" (Job 8:2). Bildad insists that God neither perverts judgment nor distorts justice. Since God does not cast away the upright, he will again one day fill Job's mouth with laughter. But Job has another question to raise: "How can a man be justified before God? Should one wish to contend with him, he could not answer him once in a thousand times" (Job 9:2-3). God is not a man like himself, observes Job, that Job should answer him, that he and God should come together in judgment. "Are not the days of my life few?" he concludes. "Let me alone, that I may recover a little before I go whence I shall not return, to the land of darkness and of gloom."

Zophar, Job's third friend, begins his remarks in much the same way that we have heard before: "Should not the man of many words be answered, or must the garrulous man necessarily be right? Shall your babblings keep men silent, and shall you deride and no one give rebuke?" (Job 10:2-3). Quite forthrightly Zophar wishes that God would speak so that Job would learn that God will make him answer for his guilt. "Can you penetrate the designs of God? Dare you vie with the perfection of the Almighty?" God sees men's iniquities; if Job would set his heart aright and remove all iniquity from his conduct, he might stand firm and unafraid. It is only the wicked who are cut off from God, with no hope for escape.

Job's next reply is filled with sarcasm: "No doubt you are the intelligent folk, and with you wisdom shall die! But I have intelligence as well as you, for who does not know such things as these?" (Job 12:2-3). We are now drawing close to the end of the first series of dialogues, and Job's comments are quite extended. He insists that what his friends know, he also knows. But it is not they with whom he wishes to discuss matters: it is with the Almighty. "I wish to reason with God," he says. He wishes that his friends would be altogether silent: "Is it for God that you speak falsehood? Is it for him that you utter deceit? Is it for him that you show partiality? Do you play advocate on behalf of God?" (Job 13:7-8). Since his friends have hinted broadly that Job must have sinned, he asks that they tell him what those sins are: "What are my faults and my sins? My misdeeds and my sins make known to me!"

All of the speeches are well worth our reading, but we shall here hurry on to the speaker who follows upon the third cycle of speeches, a younger man named Elihu. "He was angry with Job for considering himself rather than God to be in the right. He was angry also with the three friends because they had not found a good answer and had not condemned Job" (Job 32:3). When Elihu begins to speak, we detect a certain irony: "I am young and you are very old; therefore I held back and was afraid to declare to you my knowledge. Days should speak, I thought, and many years teach wisdom!" (Job 32:6-7). Elihu reprimands Job for having averred he is clean, without transgression, innocent, without guilt. He is upset, too, that Job has said that God invents pretexts against Job and that God reckons Job as his enemy. God does speak, insists Elihu, though often one does not perceive it. Surely God cannot act wickedly, the Almighty cannot violate justice. Is it right to say, "I am right, rather than God"?

Perhaps the most important thing that Elihu points out to Job is the power of God: "Behold, God is sublime in his power. What teacher is there like him? Who prescribes for him his conduct, or who can say, 'You have done wrong'?" (Job 36:22-23). Indeed, as we come toward the end of Elihu's appearance, it is clear that much that the young man has declared is a getting-ready, as it were, for the subsequent chapters in which God himself appears and speaks.

The final chapters of Job contain mostly the words of God, asking Job questions to which there is but one answer. If the power of God seems to be unduly emphasized, is it perhaps to make clear to Job that to be born into the human race is to be born simultaneously into the problem of suffering and evil, matters of which God surely knows, yet is willing to tolerate for reasons unknown to humans? No one questions that the hippopotamus and the crocodile are controllable only by God; God's mention of them prompts Job to say that he ought to have kept his hand over his mouth: how can mortal beings question him who is responsible for the entire universe?

Yet, in the long run, Job comes off far better than the three friends of Job. Job could not explain his misfortune and hated every minute of it, yet never believed that he was being punished for sins he had not committed. Job's friends, on the other hand, insisted that he must have done something, else he would never have fallen heir to so many ills. According to their thinking, each new tragedy in the life of Job was traceable to some sinfulness on his part, even though Job pleaded "not guilty" in each instance.

As we contemplate the argument of the story and listen carefully to the observations of the several characters in the drama (the book is more like a play than a story), the reply of "the Satan" at the beginning may be seen to contain more truth than is at once evident. Recall that God had asked Satan whence he came; the reply was, "From roaming the earth and patrolling it." One device in patrolling the earth can easily be the effort to persuade "Jobs" — good-living people in every corner of the earth — that whatever misfortune comes their way stems from "God getting even." Steadfastly Job resisted that suggestion. He was far more willing to acknowledge the mystery of suffering than to succumb to glib explanations for its existence. What a great lesson the Book of Job has to offer each of us as we experience, from time to time, suffering whose origin we can hardly explain.

11

I WILL SAY WHAT MY GOD TELLS ME

I n reading Sacred Scripture there are times when you have to pause, at least briefly, to consider the context in which a given story is told. Divorced from surrounding circumstances, stories can easily lose their flavor; on the contrary, when you have a lively grasp of certain details, even a single event can prove most meaningful.

Surely this is the case when you come upon the campaign against Ramoth-Gilead in the First Book of Kings or in the Second Book of Chronicles. Both books carry the story, well worth investigating; but whether you read the Kings account or that in Chronicles, a few details need to be added.

After the death of King Solomon, it will be recalled, his son Rehoboam succeeded to the throne. Approached by representatives of northern tribes who asked that their burdens be somewhat lightened, the new king replied harshly, prompting the northern tribes to secede from Rehoboam's governance and to form a new kingdom of their own, which became known as the kingdom of Israel. Rehoboam's kingdom (henceforth known as Judah) was now often at odds with Israel, and during the next several decades we read more of strife between the two kingdoms than of amicable relationships.

In the year 873 B.C.E., Jehoshaphat became king of Judah, and just a few years later, in 869, Ahab succeeded to the throne of Israel. We learn subsequently that the two new monarchs are related, and after some years Jehoshaphat went down to Ahab at Samaria, the capital of Israel. Ahab offered numerous sheep and oxen to his guest, after the manner of kings, but not simply to show his hospitality. At that time Israel was at peace with its northern neighbor, Syria, and Ahab was anxious to take the prize city of Ramoth-Gilead for himself. In offering Jehoshaphat gifts, therefore, Ahab asks his guest: "Will you come with me to fight against Ramoth-Gilead?" "You and I are one," replies the king of Judah, "your people and my people as well. We will be with you in battle" (2 Chronicles 18:3). Jehoshaphat goes on, however, to ask Ahab to consult the Lord, another way of suggesting that the king of Israel call in his prophets to discern their sentiments concerning his resolution to attack Ramoth-Gilead.

It is difficult for us to imagine a king having four hundred prophets at his disposal, but both the account in 1 Kings and that in 2 Chronicles tell the reader that four hundred prophets were at hand to give King Ahab advice on the battle. "Go up," the prophets cry in unison, "the Lord will give it over to the king." Jehoshaphat is just a bit suspicious of this unanimity it would seem, and he inquires of Ahab whether or not there is another prophet whom the two kings might consult. "There is still another," replies Ahab, "whom we may consult, but I hate him, for he prophesies not good but always evil about me. That is Micaiah, son of Imlah" (2 Chronicles 18:7). King Jehoshaphat expresses regret that Ahab would speak of evil against himself, and the king of Israel proceeds to send for Micaiah. Meanwhile, the four hundred prophets perform for the two kings, and one of them, Zedekiah, fashions iron horns for himself, declaring: "The Lord says, 'With these you shall gore Aram (Syria) until you have destroyed them.'" The other prophets present also encourage the two kings, telling them to go up to Ramoth-Gilead, assured of victory.

The messenger who went in search of Micaiah found him and said to him: "Look now, the prophets unanimously predict good for the king. Let your word, like each of theirs, predict good." "As the Lord lives," answered Micaiah, "I will say what my God tells me" (2 Chronicles 18:12-13). Micaiah now reaches the two kings and Ahab asks whether or not he and Jehoshaphat ought go up to Ramoth-Gilead. "Go up and succeed," cries Micaiah. "They will be delivered into your power." King Ahab was suspicious, however, perhaps because he had dealt with Micaiah on previous occasions. "How many times must I adjure you to tell me nothing but the truth in the name of the Lord?" asks Ahab. Then comes Micaiah's reply:

> I see all Israel scattered on the mountains, like sheep
> without a shepherd, and the Lord saying, "These have
> no master! Let each of them go back home in peace."
>
> (2 Chronicles 18:16)

Ahab is furious and exclaims to Jehoshaphat: "Did I not tell you that he prophesies no good about me, but only evil?" But Micaiah had not finished:

> Therefore hear the word of the Lord: I saw the Lord
> seated on his throne, with the whole host of heaven
> standing by to his right and to his left. The Lord asked:
> "Who will deceive Ahab, king of Israel, so that he will
> go up and fall at Ramoth-Gilead?" And one said this,
> another that, until a spirit came forward and presented
> himself to the Lord, saying, "I will deceive him." The

Lord asked, "How?" He answered, "I will go forth and
become a lying spirit in the mouths of all his prophets."
The Lord agreed: "You shall succeed in deceiving him.
Go forth and do this." So now the Lord has put a lying
spirit in the mouths of these your prophets, but the Lord
himself has decreed evil against you.

(2 Chronicles 18:18-22)

Zedekiah, among others, objected, and slapped Micaiah on
the cheek, asking which way the spirit went when it left Zedekiah
to go to Micaiah. King Ahab is furious and gives orders for Micaiah
to be imprisoned until Ahab returns safely. "If ever you return in
safety," objects Micaiah, "the Lord has not spoken through me."
Off went the two kings, and before the day had ended Ahab had
been killed in battle.

How appropriate this story in a culture in which following
the crowd seems the appropriate way to live your life. Fashions,
speech, modes of recreation: these and a host of other considerations all too easily are governed not by the invitation of the Lord
Jesus to follow him, but by the whim of the multitude. Father
Raymond Brown has somewhere written that no matter what else
discipleship means in the Gospel, above all else it signifies to be
"with Jesus." The question that surfaces for each of us is: Is my life
style one that is "with Jesus"?

In the earliest stages of Christianity, according to the Acts of
the Apostles, God's Holy Spirit, promised by Jesus during the days
of his incarnation, appeared in the form of fiery tongues and filled
all who were assembled with a holy Spirit that made possible the
gift of tongues. When some of those listening accused the apostles
of being drunk, Peter, you will recall, explained that what had transpired was the fulfillment of the prophecy of Joel. Peter, like

Micaiah, was saying what God told him to say. At a later juncture, Stephen, chosen to be a deacon, filled with grace and power, worked great signs and wonders among the people. Accused of saying things against the temple and the law, Stephen was seized and brought before the Sanhedrin. His lengthy discourse, narrated in the seventh chapter of Acts, is again exemplary of a disciple who spoke what God wanted him to say. When Philip, another disciple, fell in with a eunuch returning from Jerusalem and was questioned about a text the Ethiopian was reading from the prophet Isaiah, "Philip opened his mouth and, beginning with this scriptural passage, proclaimed Jesus to him" (Acts 8:35). Again one sees a disciple saying what God has prompted him to say. Times without number in Acts and in his epistles we hear Paul speaking what he believes the Lord has given him to say, even to the point of reprimanding Peter for what Paul believes is a lack of forthrightness concerning Christian practices.

The apostles, then, walk in the footsteps of the genuine prophets of the Hebrew Scriptures, speaking in behalf of the Lord and fearlessly setting forth what they believe the Lord wishes them to say. What about ourselves? The word prophet derives from two tiny roots, *pro*, in behalf of, and *fan*, to speak. The prophet of the Hebrew Scriptures, then, was one who spoke out in behalf of God. To be prophetic meant not so much foretelling the future, though that often was involved in what the prophet had to say. But even more than that, prophecy implied speaking out for God in season and out of season, and most often it meant saying things which people were not anxious to listen to. Each of us must ask the question: How prophetic am I? If I am to exercise the role of disciple, that is, to be with Jesus, it is essential that I be ready to speak those things that God wants me to say. How can I know those things?

However often we consider the life of the spirit, we come back to the need for prayer, for contemplation, for dialog with the Father. Without communication with Father, Son and Holy Spirit, it is all too easy to speak simply our own mind, regardless of lack of depth in what I say. If, on the other hand, we are given to serious prayer, serious conversation, so to speak, with the Maker of heaven and earth, there is every possibility that speech will be governed by the outcome of Godly dialog, reflecting our meditation.

Micaiah, as we have seen, was open to all kinds of opposition because of his refusal to go along with the four hundred prophets who kept telling King Ahab what he wanted to hear. Ahab was determined to seize Ramoth-Gilead while he had the chance. After all, he was ostensibly at peace with Syria, and since Ramoth-Gilead was really under Syrian control, now seemed the perfect time to invade the city and take it for himself — with the enemy hopefully sleeping. The prophets were canny people and knew the sentiments of the king: why say anything unfavorable, anything the king did not want to hear? The messenger who was dispatched to bring Micaiah before the two kings — Jehoshaphat and Ahab — also was a canny fellow: why upset the apple cart by saying something to Ahab that would upset him? But Micaiah is the genuine prophet: he will not be duped, neither will he fall in with the crowd simply to tickle the ears of the king. His lot, of course, was imprisonment; but for him that was far better than violating the word of the Lord, that precious inspiration that gives the satisfaction of knowing that you are moving in honesty, in accord with what God wishes.

"Leave all and follow me," said Jesus. Following him means attending to the voice of conscience, that tiny whispering that assured the prophet Elijah hiding in the cleft of the rock that the Lord God was truly present to him. So may the Lord be ever present to each of us as we strive to say what our God tells us.

12

I WILL MAKE A NEW COVENANT

ew calls in the Hebrew Scriptures seem more dramatic than that of the prophet Jeremiah. Not only was he known to God before being formed in his mother's womb: he was moreover dedicated to God before his birth — dedicated, of course, by the Lord God himself. This meant that God had chosen him for the office of prophecy, which Jeremiah was reluctant to accept. Quite probably he already realized how poorly accepted the prophets were who had gone before him — Elijah and Amos, for example. But the Lord was insistent, even placing in Jeremiah's mouth the words of the Lord. It is thus not strange to read over and again in his prophecy: "The word of the Lord came to me."

Early in his prophetic career Jeremiah learned to deal with symbols — rich symbols — communicated to him by the God who chose him. At the end of the very first chapter of the prophecy a question is addressed to the prophet: "What do you see, Jeremiah?" "I see a branch of the watching tree," replied the prophet. The Lord confirms the prophet's reply, telling him:

"Well have you seen, for I am watching to fulfill my word." What is that word? A second symbol helps clarify the first:

A second time the word of the Lord came to me with
the question: "What do you see?" "I see a boiling cauldron," I replied, "that appears from the north." And from
the north, said the Lord to me, evil will boil over upon
all the earth in the land.   (Jeremiah 1:13-14)

Through the use of two simple symbols the Lord God has
unfolded to the prophet what is to be, in a sense, the burden of
Jeremiah's life.

In 721 B.C.E., Samaria, the capital of the northern kingdom
of Israel, had fallen to the Assyrians, and countless people were
carried off into what people would later call the diaspora. Jeremiah,
living in Judah, the southern kingdom, had surely known of this,
for his prophesying takes place only a century after that event.
What, then, the prophet may have wondered to himself, is the Lord
watching? And what is that northern cauldron that is boiling over?
The Lord is watching Judah, with whom he is ill pleased because
of her infidelity. Several hundred years earlier God had revealed
to King David, through the court prophet Nathan, that he would
fix a place for his people so that they might dwell without distur-
bance, and that the house of David and his kingdom would endure
forever. But the descendants of David's household had not been
loyal to the Lord, and although prophet after prophet had been
sent to help the Chosen People return to their God, their turning
away had persisted. Almost in sheer desperation now, God has been
watching to fulfill his word, a word designed to bring his people
back to him eventually, whatever the cost of the suffering that must
be endured before a return to God is made. Thus the boiling cauldron from the north — Babylon.

As in our own day and age political fortunes shift from time
to time, so it was in the days of Jeremiah. The mighty power of

Assyria that had proven such a scourge to the northern kingdom of Israel, effecting the collapse of Samaria, has now been brought to term by a still mightier power, Babylon. The rulers of that kingdom were able to perceive quite easily the tenuous position of Judah, once Israel had fallen. Now, just as the sixth century (B.C.E.) was dawning, King Nebuchadnezzar's armies would approach Judah to test the strength or weakness of Jerusalem, to discover whether or not it was ripe for plucking.

Jeremiah cannot know this at the time God asks him what he sees; but before long all will become clear to the prophet, and he will come to understand that the Lord God will use the armies of Babylon to purify the prophet's own people, to help bring them to a realization of who really cares for them, who really defends them. But before these matters become crystal clear, the prophet himself needs to be educated, as it were, by the Lord, and much of that education will take place through the magnificent symbols employed by God in his revelations to the prophet.

Lest we think that Jeremiah is evolving ideas purely on his own, the prophet keeps reiterating: "The word of the Lord came to me." So we hear early in the second chapter. "I remember the devotion of your youth, how you loved me as a bride, following me in the desert, in a land unknown." The Lord, of course, is the husband; the Chosen People are the youthful bride.

But long ago the bride broke her yoke: "I will not serve." Though she had been planted (metaphors shift easily in Jeremiah), she has become a spurious vine, going off faithlessly to her lovers — false gods, the gods of Baal — despite the Lord God's constant fidelity. Now the prophet uses a very earthy symbol: the people have become a lusty she-camel, snuffing the wind in her ardor.

"No beasts need tire themselves seeking her, in her month they will meet her" (Jeremiah 2:24).

If a man sends away his wife, and, after leaving him, she marries another man, does the first husband come back to her? Would not the land be wholly defiled? But you have sinned with many lovers, and yet you would return to me, says the Lord. (Jeremiah 3:1)

The image of a constant lover (the Lord God) and the wayward bride of his youth (the people he has chosen) keeps coming back to the prophet, so that he may exhort Judah to mend her ways and forsake the Baals for whom she seems to lust everlastingly.

In two separate places in the prophecy we encounter the temple Sermon, in which the prophet shows forth the Lord's disgust with a people that seems to misunderstand true worship. "The temple of the Lord, the temple of the Lord, the temple of the Lord," the prophet fairly shouts; and when his listeners inquire concerning his upsetness, he tries to explain that the temple (the great temple of Solomon, in whose courtyard the sermon is being delivered) is not, and cannot be, a security blanket for so wayward a people.

Only if you thoroughly reform your ways and your deeds; if each of you deals justly with his neighbor; if you no longer oppress the resident alien, the orphan and the widow; if you no longer shed innocent blood in this place, or follow strange gods to your own harm, will I remain with you in this place, in the land which I gave your fathers long ago and for ever. (Jeremiah 7:4-7)

The prophet goes on to say that the same fate will befall the great temple that befell the shrine at Shiloh, dear to the people before the Solomonic temple was built, but since destroyed by the Philistines. The same waywardness that had characterized the generations of the period of the Judges is present here, and the same fate that came to Shiloh will now come to the Jerusalem temple.

The reader of Jeremiah's prophecy will have already guessed that this early part of his preaching is concerned with conversion — metanoia, to use the Greek term — that must take place if Judah is to be saved. And it is precisely in this area that the prophecy can be saying much to each of us. Are we wandering off with the Baals, setting up false idols in our lives in place of the loving God from whose hand we have come? Have we, like Judah, proven ourselves a faithless bride, have we forgotten the devotion of our youth, have we shed the loyalty to the Lord God that was prominent in an earlier day? It is difficult to read Jeremiah and *not* examine ourselves, *not* realize the need for conversion in our own life.

Covenant is an important concept throughout the Hebrew Scriptures, and for the prophet Jeremiah the word has almost a magic ring.

> The men who violated my covenant and did not observe
> the terms of the agreement which they made before me,
> I will make like the calf which they cut in two, between
> whose two parts they passed. The princes of Judah and
> people, who passed between the parts of the calf, I will
> hand over, all of them, to their enemies, to those who
> seek their lives: their corpses shall be food for the birds
> of the air and the beasts of the field.
>
> (Jeremiah 34:18-20)

What is this about, the reader asks: "I will make them like the calf they cut in two, between whose two parts they passed"? But before answering that, we need to inquire into the prophet's reasons for speaking at this juncture about covenant. Jeremiah has

been speaking of a pact or agreement concerning the emancipation of slaves, a pact that Judah had first agreed to and had then
broken.

King Zedekiah, writes the prophet, had made an agreement
with all the people to issue an edict of emancipation: everyone was
to free his Hebrew slaves, male and female, so that no one should
hold a man of Judah, his brother, in slavery.

> All the princes and the others who entered the agree-
> ment consented to set free their male and female ser-
> vants, so that they should be slaves no longer. But
> though they agreed and freed them, afterward they took
> back their male and female slaves whom they had set
> free and again forced them into service.
>
> (Jeremiah 34:10-11)

The word of the Lord came to the prophet, reminding Judah
of the covenant God had made with Israel:

> Every seventh year each of you shall free his Hebrew
> brother who has sold himself to you; six years he shall
> serve you, but then you shall let him go free. Your fa-
> thers, however, did not heed or obey me. Today you
> indeed repented and did what is right in my eyes by
> proclaiming the emancipation of your brethren and
> making an agreement before me in the house that is
> named after me. But then you changed your mind and
> profaned my name by taking back your male and female
> slaves to whom you had given their freedom; you forced
> them once more into slavery.   (Jeremiah 34:14-16)

In a strange twist now, the Lord tells Jeremiah that he is about
to make Judah free — free for the sword, famine and pestilence! It

is at this juncture that we come upon the verses cited above concerning the cut or split animals: Judah has clearly broken its covenant in the matter of freeing slaves and then reneging; consequently Judah will be exposed to the fate of all people who enter upon a covenant seriously, such as that portrayed in the description of the split animals.

When the prophet speaks here of covenant, he is reminded of his great forbear, Abraham (at first, Abram), whom God called from the Fertile Crescent to Canaan, modern day Israel. "I will make of you a great nation," God said to Abram, "and I will bless you; I will make your name great so that you will be a blessing." When, somewhat later, the patriarch reminded God that he was still childless, the Lord took him outside and told him to count the stars. "Just so," God said, "will your descendants be." On that occasion Abram was told to take a three-year-old heifer, a three-year-old she-goat, a three-year-old ram, and turtle dove and a young pigeon. The larger animals Abram split in two and placed each half opposite the other.

> As the sun was about to set, a trance fell upon Abram, and a deep, terrifying darkness enveloped him. Then the Lord said to Abram: "Know for certain that your descendants shall be aliens in a land not their own, where they shall be enslaved and oppressed for four hundred years."
>
> (Genesis 15:12-13)

When the sun had set, there appeared a smoking brazier and a flaming torch, which passed between those pieces. It was on that occasion, continue the Scriptures, that God made a covenant with Abraham.

The expression, "cut a covenant," derives from the practice of cutting large animals in half, as mentioned in Jeremiah and described more fully here in Genesis. In a covenant entered upon by two parties, each of the parties normally walks between the cut animals, signifying that one's fate will resemble that of the slaughtered animals if the covenant should be broken. Abraham in his trance sees just one party moving between the split animals, namely, the smoking brazier and the flaming torch, symbolizing the Lord God ratifying the covenant he had made with his favored servant, Abraham.

Jeremiah, however, speaks in another part of his prophecy of God's willingness, despite Judah's lapses, to bring forth yet another covenant, a new covenant.

> The days are coming, says the Lord, when I will make a new covenant with the house of Israel and the house of Judah. It shall not be like the covenant I made with their fathers the day I took them by the hand to lead them forth from the land of Egypt; for they broke my covenant and I had to show myself the master, says the Lord. I will place my law within them, and write it upon their hearts; I will be their God, and they shall be my people. (Jeremiah 31:31-33)

God's new covenant has been fulfilled most perfectly in the Person of God's beloved Son, Jesus Christ, and each disciple of Jesus who wants to follow him genuinely will hearken to the exhortations heard throughout the Book of Jeremiah. The redemptive death of Jesus "effects the new and definitive covenant renewal awaited by Israel. It would be a time of forgiveness, an experience that the Son of Man had already brought through his mission of compassion for those broken by sin" (Donald Senior, *The Passion of Jesus in the Gospel of Mark*, page 61). What greater satisfaction than to hear that the covenant has been written in one's heart? "I will make a new covenant."

13

I WAS NO PROPHET

The golden age of prophecy in Israel began in the eighth century Before the Common Era and continued until about the fourth century B.C.E. During that time God raised up extraordinary spokespersons who conveyed to the Chosen People both hopeful messages and warnings, in an effort to have the people remain loyal to God and, if they went astray, to return to him and to the covenant effected centuries before at Mount Sinai under the leadership of the great Moses.

We sometimes hear the expression, "non-writing prophets," and, conversely, "writing prophets." The former would include such persons as Nathan, who served as court prophet under King David, and both Elijah and Elisha, who have left behind them no written records bearing their names. Isaiah, on the other hand, and Jeremiah and Hosea and Amos, along with a number of others, are referred to as writing prophets because books bearing their names appear in the Hebrew Scriptures (or Old Testament).

Among the writing prophets of the eighth century B.C.E. we find Amos, who with Isaiah, Hosea and Micah stands at the beginning of the golden age of prophecy. If we recall that in 721 B.C.E., Samaria, the capital of the northern kingdom of Israel, fell to the

Assyrians, the mission of Amos will assume an importance that rightly belongs to it. At the very outset of his prophecy Amos identifies himself: "The words of Amos, a shepherd from Tekoa, which he received in vision concerning Israel, in the days of Uzziah, king of Judah, and in the days of Jeroboam, son of Joash, king of Israel..." (Amos 1:1). Uzziah, also known in Sacred Scripture as Azariah, ruled Judah from about 783 to 742 B.C.E.; the Jeroboam of whom Amos speaks is Jeroboam II, whose reign in Israel lasted from about 786 to 746 B.C.E. It is important to note that Amos does not identify himself as a prophet, but rather as a shepherd. Noteworthy, too, is Tekoa, located not in Israel, but in Judah.

The book gets underway with a series of judgments that the Lord has made upon a number of nations. Only after six other nations have been mentioned does the prophet come to address Judah:

> Thus says the Lord:
> For three crimes of Judah, and for four,
>   I will not revoke my word:
> Because they spurned the word of the Lord,
>   and did not keep his statutes;
> Because the lies which their fathers followed
>   have led them astray,
> I will send fire upon Judah,
>   to devour the castles of Jerusalem.   (Amos 2:4-5)

That is followed at once by a longer prophecy against Israel:

> Thus says the Lord:
> For three crimes of Israel, and for four,
>   I will not revoke my word;

> Because they sell the just man for silver,
>   and the poor man for a pair of sandals.
> They trample the heads of the weak
>   into the dust of the earth,
>   and force the lowly out of the way.
> Son and father go to the same prostitute,
>   profaning my holy name.   (Amos 2:6-7)

The prophecy against Israel continues at some length, and although eight nations have now been named, by far the longest of the utterances of Amos is made respecting Israel. One reading the prophecy for the first time might not take particular note of this, but as the words of Amos continue, we realize that the burden of the book is, indeed, Israel.

A series of rhetorical questions stands at the beginning of the third chapter: Do two walk together unless they have agreed? Does a lion roar in the forest when it has no prey? The questions continue, and the reply to each question (that must be supplied by the reader) soon lets us know the direction in which Amos' words are moving. Both women and men are addressed caustically as the fourth chapter of the prophecy opens, in which the women of Samaria are addressed as "cows of Bashan," who cry out to their husbands: "Bring drink for us!"

Bashan was a mountain on which were raised fine and very stout cattle; there is nothing flattering in Amos' speaking to the women as cows of Bashan. When we read of the women calling out to their husbands for a drink, we have the impression of a society of well-to-do people who have slight concern for the poverty and want around them. That impression is emphasized as the prophet goes on to address the citizenry of Israel: "Come to Bethel and sin, to Gilgal, and sin the more!" Only later on in the prophecy do we realize that it is precisely in Bethel that the prophet is speaking, for it is to Bethel, where the king and his court worship, that the prophet has been directed by God.

Like all of Sacred Scripture, the prophecies are far more than simple historical records. The proverbial two-edged sword (that sacred writ is) aims to penetrate the person reading or hearing as much as the person about whom the account speaks. We are prompted to ask ourselves: Am I a cow of Bashan, careless of the needy about me? Am I coming to Bethel or Gilgal or wherever to sin? Or is my life conscious of the covenant made by God with myself at the moment of my baptism, when I was first invested with the light that is Jesus Christ?

An expression that we find now and then in the prophets is "the day of the Lord." The general sense of the words seems to imply that when the day of the Lord comes, the Lord God is going to render justice to those who have been opprobrious to the Chosen People. Amos leaps on this: "Woe to those who yearn for the day of the Lord! What will this day of the Lord mean for you? Darkness and not light!" (Amos 5:18). Let not the resident of Israel think, then, that the day of the Lord is going to take care of things; on the contrary, those who self-righteously look to the day of the Lord will find themselves in the wrong corner! The prophet speaks of "lying upon beds of ivory," stretching comfortably on couches, eating lambs taken from the flock, drinking wine from bowls, and wanton revelry. All of this will go, for the Lord is raising up a nation that will oppress Israel.

After a series of visions — locusts, fire, and the plummet — in each of which Amos begs the Lord to spare Israel, we come upon a confrontation between Amaziah, high priest of the temple at Bethel, and Amos, in which we discover just how the man from Tekoa happened to be prophesying in the city of the king's temple.

Amaziah sends word to the king (Jeroboam II): "Amos has conspired against you within Israel; the country cannot endure all his words. For this is what Amos says: 'Jeroboam shall die by the sword, and Israel shall surely be exiled from the land'" (Amos 7:10-11). The priest then addresses himself to Amos, telling him to be gone: "Off with you, visionary, flee to the land of Judah! There earn your bread by prophesying, but never again prophesy in Bethel; for it is the king's sanctuary and a royal temple."

Calling Amos a visionary (or prophet) and telling him to go back home to prophesy, was too much for Amos. "I was no prophet," he replied, "nor have I belonged to a company of prophets; I was a shepherd and a dresser of sycamores." Recall that at the very beginning of the prophecy Amos identified himself as being from Tekoa, a city located not in Israel, but in Judah. Hence Amaziah's dismissal of the prophet, in effect saying, "Go home and prophesy there if you want to, but do not prophesy here in the city of the king's temple." Mistakenly, Amaziah believed Amos to be a professional prophet, one who regularly spoke for the Lord. At least, thought Amaziah, he must belong to a school of prophets, spoken of now and then in the Scriptures. But Amos will accept neither designation: I was no prophet, he insists; "The Lord took me from following the flock, and said to me, 'Go, prophesy to my people Israel.'" Amos' vocation, then, was not that of prophet: he was simply minding his flocks and his trees when directed by the Lord to go to the northern kingdom of Israel and to prophesy in the temple of Bethel.

The vocation of Amos has not ceased to exist: how often in life we are asked to speak out in situations that we never anticipated. We need not be given to prophecy, we need not have a vocation normally associated with preaching. The Lord may put his hand where he will and may ask any of us to speak in his behalf.

That, after all, is what prophecy means: speaking out for another, and when God is specifically involved, speaking out for God. Such speaking out may not always be welcome. At a later date Jesus would say that a prophet is recognized everywhere except in his own country. In Amos' case, he was not welcome outside Judah; but then, we remind ourselves, Amos was not a prophet in the usual sense of the word. He was, as he insists, a keeper of sheep and sycamores: I was no prophet!

The encounter that took place between Amos and Amaziah wound up with a prediction by the man from Tekoa: the wife of Amaziah would become a harlot in the city, said Amos, and the priest's sons and daughters would die by the sword. All of this may have seemed to Amaziah a vengeful retort by the prophet, but a tragic end awaited Samaria and the entire northern kingdom. In 721 B.C.E. the Assyrians attacked the northern capital (Samaria), and it is not difficult to imagine the fate that eventually overtook Bethel as well. Countless numbers of the Chosen People were deported, never again to return to their homeland.

Happily, at the end of the Book of Amos we come upon a hopeful prophecy, spoken by the Lord through the keeper of sheep and sycamore tress: "I will bring about the restoration of my people Israel; they shall rebuild and inhabit their ruined cities, plant vineyards and drink the wine."

14

I WILL LEAD HER INTO THE DESERT

ew books of Sacred Scripture have a more dramatic opening than the Book of Hosea: "Go, take a harlot wife and harlot's children...." The prophet, obedient to God's word, weds Gomer, and she bears him a son.

> Give him the name Jezrael,
> for in a little while
> I will punish the house of Jehu
> for the bloodshed at Jezrael
> And bring to an end the kingdom
> of the house of Israel.　　　　(Hosea 1:4)

Gomer again conceives, this time a daughter, to whom the name Lo-ruhama is given: "I no longer feel pity for the house of Israel." When Gomer conceives a third time, a son is born: "Give him the name Lo-ammi, for you are not my people, and I will not be your God."

We recognize immediately, of course, that strange ground is afoot, and that this is no ordinary story. Before long it becomes clear that we are dealing with a parable: Gomer is Israel and Hosea is the Lord God. Gomer — Israel — is faithless but Hosea — God — is constant. We gather the impression as the text moves along that despite Hosea's devoted love, Gomer is always ready to return to her former lovers. At length Hosea says that he will allure her, lead her into the desert. "She shall respond there as in the days of her youth, when she came up from the land of Egypt" (Hosea 2:17).

The more we read, the more do we become enmeshed in the difficult alliance that has been created from the beginning of the story. The more we see the parallels that are being drawn, the more we come to appreciate the genuineness of God's love for his people and the extraordinary lengths to which he has gone, and continues to go, to help his people maintain some kind of fidelity to himself. Part way through the book the metaphor changes: the Lord God is no longer the steadfast husband, but rather a devoted father; Israel, no longer the wife, is now a child, whom God loved and whom he called out of Egypt.

> The more I called them,
> the farther they went from me,
> Sacrificing to the Baals
> and burning incense to idols.
> Yet it was I who taught Ephraim to walk,
> who took them in my arms;
> I drew them with human cords,
> with bands of love;
> I fostered them like one
> who raises an infant to his cheeks;
> Yet, though I stooped to feed my child,
> they did not know that I was their healer.
>
> (Hosea 11:2-4)

Israel and the desert are almost synonymous terms throughout the Exodus, the greatest period of Israel's history. It was in the desert that God taught the people, indeed, made them really God's people, and gave them a solidarity that they had not known in Egypt. It was the Lord God who fed her, who protected her from her enemies, who brought her to the Mount of Sinai to effect a covenant that would forever after bind his children to himself. "With an undying love I have loved them."

We do not find it strange, therefore, that Hosea leads Gomer into the desert, for it is there that she can learn again the enormous love that Hosea has for her. The usual distractions that a person encounters in everyday life are absent in the desert. There in the desert Gomer will be able to hear Hosea when he speaks, she will be able to understand when he explains the profundity of his love and care. In the desert he can remind her of the original covenant of love and remind her of the relentless love that has been expended on her. There in the desert Hosea can help Gomer to cast aside her false lovers — the Baals — and can exhort her to devote herself to him who truly loves her, her husband.

The prophet tells Gomer that he will give her the vineyards she had, a reference, of course, to Israel itself, whom God planted as a farmer plants a precious vine. That vine at one time extended from the River (the Euphrates) to the Sea (the Mediterranean). But the vinedressers were at times careless of their charge, and the Great Vintner — the Lord God — must again give himself to the cultivation of his vine, lest it bring forth (as in Isaiah's "Song of the Vineyard") wild grapes.

Again we need to stop in order to reflect on Gomer and Hosea and the desert, and to ask ourselves about the desert in our own life today. Is my life preoccupied with so many concerns that I have little time for the desert, little time to move away from the hubbub that threatens at times to lessen my vision of the closeness of the Almighty? To go into the desert means to put ourselves quite completely in the arms of the all-loving Father in order to learn afresh the lessons of the Exodus, the lessons of Sinai. Recall the great Elijah, pursued by Jezebel, fleeing south into the Negeb, on down into Sinai. It was needful for him, he felt, to hear the Lord God reaffirm the covenant, to reassure Elijah that his prophetic voice was indeed speaking out for the Lord when Elijah challenged, on Mount Carmel, the prophets of Baal. We, too, must challenge the false gods that all too easily insert themselves into our lives, and to accomplish that there is perhaps no more effective place than the desert, that area that permits us to focus honestly and without pretense on the intimate relationship that the Lord has established between himself and ourselves.

In the Book of Exodus we read: "See, I am sending an angel before you, to guard you on the way and bring you to the place I have prepared. Be attentive to him and hear his voice" (Exodus 23:20-21). In the prophecy of Malachi, the final book of the Old Testament, we read: "Lo, I am sending my messenger to prepare the way before me" (Malachi 3:1). And in Isaiah we find the passage: "A voice cries out: In the desert prepare the way of the Lord" (Isaiah 40:3). These three texts seem to come together at the very beginning of Mark's Gospel, when, after announcing the Gospel of Jesus Christ, the evangelist writes:

> Behold, I am sending my messenger ahead of you to prepare your way. A voice of one crying out in the desert, "Prepare the way of the Lord, make straight his paths."   (Mark 1:23)

Mark then goes on to speak of the appearance of John the

Baptist appearing in the desert, proclaiming a baptism of repentance for the forgiveness of sins. Many people were going out to him, Mark continues, and were being baptized by him in the Jordan River as they acknowledged their sins. Mark further describes the dress and the diet of John: he was clothed in camel's hair, with a belt around his waist. He fed on locusts and wild honey.

The picture portrayed here is important because it gives us some idea of the nature of this first prophet to appear in the New Testament. The golden age of prophecy (about 750 to 350 B.C.E.) had long since ended in the Hebrew Scriptures; yet we are not to think that prophecy has disappeared. Where prophets of old have left off, John will now take up. Characteristically, he is easily identifiable as a prophet not only by what he says, but by the food he eats and by the clothing he wears as well. It is not accidental, either, that John appears at the edge of the desert, a region dear to those who had been freed from bondage in Egypt centuries before and who had found their way to the Promised Land only through their wandering in the desert. John, then, clearly represents the best of prophecy as the Chosen People had come to know it through the centuries; and when John spoke, the language he used was not far removed from that which had fallen from the lips of the great voices of Isaiah and Jeremiah and Ezekiel.

To the crowds who came out to be baptized, John said, ""You brood of vipers! Who warned you to flee from the coming wrath? Produce good fruits as evidence of your repentance" (Luke 3:7-8). When the crowds asked John what they should do, he replied: "Whoever has two cloaks should share with the person who has none. And whoever has food should do likewise" (Luke 3:11). When tax collectors came and asked what they should do, his reply was brief and unequivocal: "Stop collecting more than what is prescribed." To soldiers inquiring of him he replied: "Do not practice extortion, do not falsely accuse anyone, and be satisfied with your wages" (Luke 3:13-14).

When our Savior comes to John to be baptized, he quickly identifies with John. Indeed, in Mark's Gospel, the language used by Jesus when he returns to Galilee after being baptized, resembles that of John: "The kingdom of God is at hand. Repent, and believe in the gospel" (Mark 1:15). Jesus, therefore, recognizes the importance of prophecy, the need to speak out for God, and, in the same breath, the cogency of the desert which served as the training grounds for Elijah, who preceded by a century the golden age of prophecy. The desert will not be foreign to our Savior: shortly after his baptism by John, he is led into the desert, where he remains for forty days, to be tempted by Satan.

Small wonder that Hosea led Gomer into the desert. Where, if not there, would she come to understand the depth of his love for her? With us, too, the need for the desert is always present if we would keep our values in perspective. All around us is the temptation to accept ways that do not accord with discipleship. It is the desert that helps us realize the ways of the Lord Jesus.

Finally, recall the desert imagery presented in the second part of Isaiah's prophecy, that part of the prophecy that is often spoken of as Second Isaiah or Deutero-Isaiah. The Chosen People have been in exile now for fifty years or more, when suddenly their release is about to be accomplished by Cyrus, king of Persia, who has overcome Babylon. Second Isaiah sees the new deliverance about to happen as a new or second Exodus, greater in many ways than the first.

> In the desert prepare the way of the Lord!
> Make straight in the wasteland a highway for our God!
> Every valley shall be filled in,

> Every mountain and hill shall be made low...
> Then the glory of the Lord shall be revealed,
>   and all mankind shall see it together,
>   for the mouth of the Lord has spoken.
>
> (Isaiah 40:3-5)

For Second Isaiah the desert will be redeemed Israel's way to salvation, that is, to its return to Judah and Jerusalem. His imagination is fired up as he contemplates his fellow-exiles leaving their Babylonian bondage to return to their homeland. And how will this be accomplished? In the same way Israel's release from Egypt had been achieved: through the desert!

When we speak of the desert and of the prophets who were so intimately connected with the desert in their very thinking, we cannot forget the words spoken by Zechariah, father of John the Baptist, in a canticle that has come to form part of the Church's official Morning Prayer: "You, child, will be called prophet of the Most High, for you will go before the Lord to prepare his ways, to give his people knowledge of salvation through the forgiveness of their sins" (Luke 1:76-77). Each of us, in a sense, is to be a prophet of the Most High, each of us, like the prophets of old, is to go before the Lord to prepare the way for him.

At the very end of the Book of Hosea, words of great solace are set forth, and these may serve to conclude what is here set down concerning the eternal quest for requited love that runs from one end of the Sacred Scriptures to the other:

> Let those who are wise understand these things;
>   let those who are prudent know them.
> Straight are the paths of the Lord,
>   in them the just walk....

15

MENE, TEKEL, PERES

While some books of the Hebrew Scriptures give us a picture of events that took place in a given period of Israel's history, others veil the time frame in which they are written, giving us the impression that the events narrated belong to an era that is somewhat fictional. The Book of Daniel is representative of the latter category of book, and is one of the late books of the Hebrew Scriptures.

The pretended scene is Babylon and the king is Nebuchadnezzar. The supposed time is the sixth century Before the Common Era, a period of great hardships for God's Chosen People. The sacred author seems clearly to have in mind the period of the Exile (587 B.C.E.), when Babylon advanced on Jerusalem, burned the house of the Lord, the palace of the king, and all the large houses of Jerusalem. The walls that surrounded Jerusalem were torn down, and hundreds of the residents of Jerusalem were taken captive and carted off to Babylon, including King Zedekiah, whose sons were killed in his presence and whose eyes were subsequently blinded by his captors. Perhaps it is only the Book of Lamentations that does justice to the cruel suffering endured in that sad period of Israel's history.

As the Book of Daniel opens, young sons of Israel are being selected, men of talent and culture, to enhance the court of the Chaldeans in Babylon. Among those chosen are Daniel and three of his friends, Hananiah, Mishael and Azariah. An early test of their loyalty to the Law handed down from Mount Sinai comes when they are invited to accept Chaldean foods. Daniel and his friends persuade the chief chamberlain to conduct a test: let them observe their regular diet, and at the end of ten days compare their appearance with that of those who have eaten from the royal table. At the specified time, Daniel and his companions appeared in better condition than the others, and they were consequently permitted to observe their regular fast.

From this point forward in the Book of Daniel, matters are not always well ordered. The second and fourth chapters tell of dreams experienced by Nebuchadnezzar, and in both instances Daniel, like the patriarch Joseph of an earlier millennium and more, is able to interpret the king's dreams. In between those chapters we read of a plot devised by people close to the king who are resentful of Daniel and his companions. They devise a ploy that calls for the worship of a statue of the king and suggest to Nebuchadnezzar that the penalty for non-observance should be a fiery furnace for any and all offenders. We are conscious of a certain humor in the narration of this story, as the sacred writer repeats over and again the king's order that at the sound of the trumpet, flute, lyre, harp, psaltery, bagpipe, and all the other musical instruments, everyone must fall down and worship the statue of Nebuchadnezzar. The constant repetition of the names of the various instruments may well bring a smile to our lips.

Daniel's companions, whose Babylonian names are now Shadrach, Meschach and Abednego, fail to worship as directed and are duly reported to the king for their violation of the newly imposed law. The penalty, of course, is the fiery furnace, into which Daniel's three friends are presently thrown. So huge was the fire prepared for the three that the flames devoured the men who threw Shadrach, Meschach and Abednego into the furnace. The three immediately began to sing in praise of God, and although the heat of the fire was increased, the men walked unscathed through the flames. To the amazement of the king, not three, but four figures were seen: "I see four men unfettered and unhurt," said the king, "walking in the fire, and the fourth looks like a son of God" (Daniel 3:92). Orders were given for the release of the men from the flames; the king now praised the God of Israel, and Shadrach, Meshach and Abednego were promoted in the province of Babylon.

In reading the Book of Daniel, we must be aware that didactic fiction has a place in Sacred Scripture and that parts of the book are illustrative of that kind of writing. That does not mean that the stories are simply stories and nothing more. Rather, it is intended that the accounts narrated will stimulate the faith of those reading and remind them, in this particular instance, that confidence in the Lord God of heaven and earth can bring one through the most difficult of circumstances.

In the fifth chapter of the book, the name of the king suddenly changes: instead of reading about Nebuchadnezzar, we now read of King Belshazzar, said to be the inheritor of the throne and the son of Nebuchadnezzar. A splendid banquet is arranged, during which sacred vessels captured from the temple in Jerusalem are used as drinking cups. In the middle of the wining and dining, writing suddenly appears on the wall, frightening the king and all present. No one is able to decipher the writing, but the queen mother, recalling Daniel's expertise in interpreting dreams during the reign of King Nebuchadnezzar, suggests that he be called. King Belshazzar promises all kinds of rewards to Daniel when he appears, but he spurns those as he offers to analyze the writing on the wall:

> This is the writing that was inscribed: MENE, TEKEL, and PERES. These words mean: MENE, God has numbered your kingdom and put an end to it. TEKEL, you have been weighed on the scales and found wanting; PERES, your kingdom has been divided and given to the Medes and Persians. (Daniel 5:25-28)

The chapter closes by informing us that that night Belshazzar, the Chaldean king, was slain.

Darius the Mede succeeds to the kingdom, and again Daniel comes into prominence. So renowned, in fact, does he become, that jealousy of his advancement prompts supervisors and satraps to devise a plot that will provoke the animus of the king with respect to Daniel. For thirty days no one is to address any god or man with a petition, except that that petition be addressed to King Darius. Daniel, as we might have guessed, continued to worship God openly and was reported to the king. The penalty was to be the lions' den, to which, regretfully, King Darius now sentences Daniel. The entire time in which Daniel is in the den is one of peace between prophet and animal, and Daniel is not touched by the lions. When King Darius discovered after a day that Daniel remained safe and untouched, he ordered Daniel brought forth from the den and had the satraps and their families thrown to the lions. "Before they reached the bottom of the pit, the lions overpowered them and crushed all their bones" (Daniel 6:25). So pleased was the king with Daniel's rescue that he published a decree ordering that the God of Daniel was to be reverenced and feared. The sixth chapter of the book concludes by informing us that Daniel fared well during the reign of Darius and also during that of Cyrus the Persian.

The second half of the Book of Daniel is quite different from the first part. Instead of didactic history, we are now faced with a series of visions, the first of which, found in the seventh chapter, is much used by the Church in her liturgy. The vision opens with Daniel experiencing a very troublesome dream during the reign of King Belshazzar, of whom the story of the handwriting on the wall was told earlier. Daniel now speaks in the first person as he recounts his dream, a vision concerning four immense beasts, each different from the others. As the beasts disappear, there springs out a horn with eyes like a man's and with a mouth that speaks arrogantly.

> As I watched, thrones were set up
>> and the Ancient One took his throne.
> His clothing was snow bright,
>> and the hair on his head was white as wool;
> His throne was flames of fire,
>> with wheels of burning fire.
> A surging stream of fire
>> went out from where he sat;
> Thousands upon thousands were ministering to him, and
>> myriads upon myriads attended him.
> As the visions during the night continued, I saw
> One like a son of man
>> coming on the clouds of heaven;
> When he reached the ancient One,
>> and was presented before him,
>> he received dominion, glory, and kingship,

Nations and people of every language serve him.
His dominion is an everlasting dominion
    that shall not be taken away,
    his kingship shall not be destroyed.

                  (Daniel 7:9-10, 13-14)

Daniel is understandably disturbed by what he sees in the vision and addresses himself to one of those present to inquire about the meaning of the vision. The four great beasts, he is told, stand for four kingdoms which shall arise on the earth. "But the holy ones of the Most High shall receive the kingship, to possess it for ever and ever" (Daniel 7:17)

In the *Jerome Biblical Commentary* we read: "In the context, the one in human form is not a real individual but a symbol. However, because in Daniel the thought of 'kingdom' often shifts imperceptibly into that of 'king,' the concept of the 'son of man' eventually shifted from a figure of speech for the theocratic kingdom into a term for the messianic king himself" (*JBC*, pp. 416-417). It is in this latter sense that the Church employs the Daniel texts over and again in celebrating feasts connected with the Person of Jesus. One sees, too, how the author of Apocalypse could have been influenced by the author of Daniel in portraying the "one who sits on the throne" and the "lamb worthy to receive glory and honor and blessing."

There are further visions in Daniel, and at the end of the book the reader encounters two stories, the first of great length, that of Susanna and the unworthy elders. Susanna, unjustly accused of adultery by two elders who, out of lust, wished her favor for themselves, is saved through the wisdom of the youthful Daniel, and the elders are themselves put to death for their evil machinations.

The final chapter narrates a story concerning Bel, an idol that was supposedly a hearty eater. Daniel's wit in discovering for the king the fallacy of belief in Bel wins him few friends. This is quickly followed by the story of a dragon to whom Daniel feeds pitch, fat and hair, killing the dragon. The result: Daniel to the lions' den. Here he is helped by the prophet Habakkuk, lifted by the crown of his head by an angel and borne to Babylon with food for Daniel in the den. As in the previous lions' den story, Daniel is spared by the lions and released by the king, who then gives over to the lions those responsible for trying to destroy Daniel.

A book so full of stories (as the Book of Daniel is) may well prompt the reader of Sacred Scripture to wonder not only about the number of tales, but also about the nature of the narratives. It is believed by many that the writer of the Book of Daniel lived in the second century B.C.E., a time fraught with overwhelming hardships and difficulties for God's Chosen People. Not unnaturally, the writer thinks back to an age that was comparable — that of the Exile of 587 B.C.E., when Jerusalem itself fell and great numbers of its residents were carried off to Babylon. What kind of spirit had to animate faithful Jews in those days? The same type of faith in God, with loyalty to the covenant, is needed in the second century, in which the writer finds himself. Daniel and his companions are illustrative of a solid confidence in God's abiding presence.

For the contemporary or modern reader, of course, the story does not stop there. What age does not see a secular approach to life battling the Wisdom of God? And who among us does not find it imperative to keep our eye fixed on a God who remains unshaken, whatever the human circumstances that surround us?

The Book of Daniel was written during an age that saw much of apocalyptic — a style of writing that concerns itself with the end of the temporal world. We are not surprised, therefore, to find passages describing visions having to do with an unseen time. Messianic currents were also present here and there in the early centuries preceding Christianity, and it is not strange that part of Daniel's visions should be seen as looking forward not simply to the end-time, but to the coming of God's specially Anointed.

Faith and trust in God, then, accompanied by a confidence that God, not man, rules the universe, are fitting dispositions with which we ought to move to the Book of Daniel.

16

THE INFANCY NARRATIVES

Dear to the heart of many a reader of the New Testament are the Gospel stories read at Christmas liturgies from the so-called Infancy Narratives of Saint Matthew and Saint Luke. Both writers are believed to have composed their Gospel accounts perhaps as much as fifteen years after Saint Mark wrote his work. While the latter introduces the reader at once into the adult life of Jesus, both Luke and Matthew contain two chapters at the very outset of their Gospel accounts concerning the earliest history of Jesus. Both writers convey to their readers matters of great interest. But the two are very different in their approaches to the incarnation of Jesus even though in certain matters, fundamental to the incarnation, they are at one.

The present writer is indebted to a volume of Father Raymond E. Brown, available to readers since the late nineteen seventies, *The Birth of the Messiah*. Father Brown's entire work is concerned with just four chapters of Sacred Scripture, chapters one and two of both Matthew and Luke. His detailed explanations have gone far to illuminate countless readers in their pursuit of knowledge concerning our Savior's infancy.

Matthew's Gospel begins with a genealogy, the genealogy of

Jesus Christ, the son of David, the son of Abraham. That very introduction tells us that Matthew is tipping his hand, so to speak, from the outset: he does not begin with Adam, as he might have done, but with "the son of David, the son of Abraham." Jesus is indeed the son of David, descended from the great king of Israel through the tribe of Judah. And since all members of Israel are descended from Abraham, the father of the Jewish race, so David, and so, too, Jesus Christ.

Matthew divides his genealogy into three sections, in each of which (Matthew tells us) are fourteen names. In the first section we find Abraham, Isaac, Jacob, Judah; Perez, Hezron, Ram, Aminadab; Nahshon, Salmon, Boaz, Obed; Jesse and David. Matthew does not interrupt the series of names here, but in a later verse he will point out that "the total number of generations from Abraham to David is fourteen generations" (Matthew 1:17).

The list now continues with Solomon, Rehoboam, Abijah, Asaph; Jehoshaphat, Joram, Uzziah, Jotham; Ahaz, Hezekiah, Manasseh, Amos; Josiah and Jeconiah. Later Matthew will observe: "From David to the Babylonian exile, fourteen generations" (Matthew 1:17). The final section of the list includes: Shealtiel, Zerubbabel, Abiud, Eliakim; Azor, Zadok, Achim, Eliud; Eleazar, Matthan, Jacob, Joseph; Jesus. In this final section, Matthew, after mentioning Joseph, writes, "the husband of Mary. Of her was born Jesus, who is called the Messiah" (Matthew 1:16). A little later he points out: "From the Babylonian exile to the Messiah, fourteen generations" (Matthew 1:17).

Several questions arise: are names generations? what about thirteen, instead of fourteen names in the third section? Father Brown, in the book already mentioned, has a fine second chapter on the Matthean Infancy Narrative, entitled "The Genealogy of Jesus." Among other matters he considers Matthew's composition of the genealogy, Matthew's introduction of women's names (they occur here and there) deliberately introduced as mothers of specific forbears of Jesus, the magic number fourteen and Matthew's ability to count! The entire section is well worth reading.

The Hebrew alphabet attaches certain numerical values to its letters, and as matters turn out, the name David has a numerical value of fourteen: the fourth letter of the alphabet, *daleth*, equals four; the sixth letter, *waw*, is valued at six; and *daleth* (again) equals four. Since vowels would not have been written out in the original Hebrew Bible, the name of David has a numerical value of fourteen. Was Matthew not really interested so much in names as in establishing fourteen for each section, in order to emphasize the connection between David and Jesus? To suggest that is not to indicate that the names are without meaning.

How, thus far, does Matthew differ from Luke? Very much indeed! Luke postpones genealogy until a later section of his Gospel, and begins the Infancy Narrative with an overall introduction to his book:

> Since many have undertaken to compile a narrative of the events that have been fulfilled among us, just as those who were eyewitnesses from the beginning and ministers of the word have handed them down to us, I too have decided, after investigating everything accurately anew, to write it down in an orderly sequence for you, most excellent Theophilus, so that you may realize the certainty of the teachings you have received.
>
> (Luke 1:1-4)

From that introduction Luke proceeds at once to the announcement of the birth of John the Baptist, a matter not considered at all in Matthew's Infancy Narrative. In Luke, this is of great importance in several ways: it serves as a kind of model for the birth story of Jesus that is to follow, and opens the way for comparisons here and there between the precursor and the Savior of mankind. Since Matthew, once he has completed the genealogy, moves on to the birth of Jesus, it will be advantageous here to move into Luke's account as he speaks of John.

The principal characters here are Zechariah and Elizabeth, man and wife, both of advanced age. The former belongs to the priestly division of Abijah and is serving his turn in priestly service as the story begins. The angel of the Lord appears to him to announce that Elizabeth will bear Zechariah a son who is to be named John. Remarkable things are prophesied by the angel concerning John, but Zechariah finds the entire experience a bit incomprehensible because of the advanced age of Elizabeth and himself. Because of his doubting, he is deprived of the faculty of speech until the time that the matters prophesied come to pass. When Zechariah emerges from the sanctuary unable to speak, people conclude that he has experienced a vision. When he returns home, Elizabeth conceives, "and she went into seclusion for five months, saying, 'So has the Lord done for me at the time when he has seen fit to take away my disgrace before others'" (Luke 1:24-25).

Matthew's account of the birth of Jesus is briefer than that of Luke, who includes an extended narration concerning the announcement of his birth. Certain differences between the two evangelists in their handling of this part of their story are worth our note. In the Gospel of Matthew, Mary is betrothed to Joseph, but "before they lived together, she was found with child through the Holy Spirit" (Matthew 1:18). The last phrase is very important, for the two evangelists, however they may differ in their overall account of matters, are in complete agreement that what takes place in the womb of Mary is the work of God's Holy Spirit. In Luke's annunciation scene, after the angel Gabriel has told Mary what God plans for her, she raises a question: "How can this be, since I have no relations with a man?" (Luke 1:34). The reply of Gabriel follows at once: "The Holy Spirit will come upon you, and the power of the Most High will overshadow you. Therefore the child to be born will be called holy, the Son of God" (Luke 1:35). When Joseph, in Matthew's Gospel, decides to divorce Mary quietly, an angel appears to him in a dream and says: "Joseph, son of David, do not be afraid to take Mary your wife into your home. For it is through the Holy Spirit that this child has been conceived in her" (Matthew 1:20). The two evangelists, therefore, are at one in expressing their belief in Mary's virginal conception of the child Jesus.

What, then, is different? In the Matthean Gospel, the revelation is made to Joseph; in Luke the word is given by the angel to Mary. Matthew concludes this part of his Infancy Narrative by noting that Joseph, having received the testimony of the angel, did as the angel commanded him and took Mary into his home. He had no relations with her until she bore a son, and he named him Jesus (Matthew 1:24-25). These remarks bring us to the conclusion of Matthew's first chapter. The chapter to follow deals with very different material, the visit of the Magi and the consequences of that visit. It will be good now, therefore, to return to Luke, to see how he proceeds with his Gospel, following the annunciation to Mary, spoken of above.

Luke's Infancy Narrative is punctuated by three songs or canticles, the first of which occurs on the occasion of Mary's visit to Elizabeth. The angel Gabriel has already made clear to Mary that Elizabeth is now in her sixth month, and this prompts Mary to leave Nazareth and to visit her kinswoman, Elizabeth. The visit, filled with appreciative love on the part of both women, concludes with

Mary's canticle: "My soul proclaims the greatness of the Lord...." At the conclusion of the canticle, says Luke, "Mary remained with her about three months and then returned to her home" (Luke 1:5b).

An account of the birth of John follows, with its accompanying story of the loosening of the tongue of Zechariah. As Mary's canticle concluded the account of her visit to Elizabeth, so now a canticle by Zechariah brings to an end the story of John's birth. Luke is now ready to present the birth of Jesus, for which the account of John's birth was a preparation. The reader does not find it strange that the birth of the Messiah should be more elaborately described than that of the precursor, John. Joseph and Mary have gone up from Nazareth to Bethlehem (according to Luke) for the enrollment prescribed by Caesar Augustus. There Mary brings forth her firstborn, and shepherds receive the good news from angels and travel to Bethlehem to see the newborn. When Mary heard from the shepherds their account of the angelic choir, she pondered these things in her heart. Almost at once Luke goes on to speak of the circumcision of Jesus and then tells of the presentation of our Savior in the temple. The third of Luke's canticles now occurs, as Simeon, a righteous and devout man, recognizes Jesus as Messiah and sings, "Now, Master, you may let your servant go in peace, according to your word..." (Luke 2:29). Anna, a widow for many decades, gives thanks to God for the child and speaks about him "to all who were awaiting the redemption of Jerusalem" (Luke 2:38).

Because the Gospel of Luke now turns to the growing child, it will be appropriate at this juncture to return to Matthew, whose account of what follows takes place while Jesus is still an infant.

It has been pointed out by certain writers that even without Matthew's first chapter, the opening of chapter two would make sense: "When Jesus was born in Bethlehem of Judah, in the days of King Herod, behold magi from the east arrived in Jerusalem, saying, 'Where is the newborn king of the Jews?'" (Matthew 2:1-2). With that initiatory sentence, the evangelist begins an account familiar to those who have experienced the Christmas season liturgies — the story of the wise men from the east who had come to worship Jesus and who, warned by an angel, returned to their home country by a way different from that on which they had come. The story involves a much-troubled Herod directing the magi to let him know the whereabouts of the king they had come to worship, so that he, too, might worship him. The massacre of the infants, of which there seems to be no account in secular history, comes about after Mary and Joseph have fled to Egypt with the child. Upon their return they go to Nazareth, Joseph having been warned in a dream not to remain in Judah. It is Matthew's only mention of Nazareth; Matthew concludes his Infancy Narrative: "He shall be called a Nazorean" (Matthew 2:23).

The term "Infancy Narrative" may seem to lose something of that meaning when we come to the final section of Luke's second chapter. There is, however, a bridge between the infancy of Jesus and the narration concerning the boy Jesus remaining behind in the Jerusalem temple: "The child grew and became strong, filled with wisdom; and the favor of God was upon him" (Luke 2:40). That single sentence brings the reader forward to the temple story of Jesus remaining there, with Joseph and Mary unaware that he was not in the caravan traveling back to Galilee. When, after retracing their steps, they find him speaking with the doctors of the Law, and Mary asks if he did not realize the grief he had caused them, our Savior speaks about the need he has to be in his Father's house. "They did not understand what he said to them. He went down with them and came to Nazareth, and was obedient to them" (Luke 2:50-51). Luke closes this part of his Gospel with the remark: "Jesus advanced in wisdom and age and favor before God and man" (Luke 2:52).

What fruitful sources of meditation are found in the Infancy Narratives! Both Luke and Matthew have made clear to all that they are speaking of God's Son, virginally conceived in the womb of Mary. At every turn, enormous faith is expressed: by Joseph, by Mary, by the parents of John the Baptist, by the magi, by Simeon and Anna, not to forget the shepherds. To read the Infancy Narratives slowly and with something of that pondering reflective of Mary is to enter upon an introduction to the life of Jesus that is incomparable. To do otherwise is to deprive ourselves of rich, prayerful experiences. As you read these narratives may you come to an ever greater understanding of how the Good News began.

17

THE KINGDOM OF HEAVEN IS AT HAND

The reader of the New Testament is never surprised in finding certain similarities in the Gospel accounts of Mark, Matthew and Luke. The three separate versions of the preaching and teaching of Jesus have not been called synoptic for nothing: there is unquestionably a relationship among them that reveals itself quite prominently and reasonably often in certain areas of the three accounts.

In each synoptic Gospel, Jesus is baptized by John the Baptist and afterwards commences his public life. Saint Luke portrays our Savior at Nazareth, where he had grown up, entering the synagogue on the sabbath and being handed a scroll of the prophet Isaiah from which to read.

> The spirit of the Lord is upon me, because he has anointed me to bring glad tidings to the poor. He has sent me to proclaim liberty to captives and recovery of sight to the blind, to let the oppressed go free, and to proclaim a year acceptable to the Lord. (Luke 4:17-19)

When our Savior had rolled up the scroll and returned it to the synagogue attendant and sat down, everyone looked intently at him. He said to them: "Today this scripture passage is fulfilled in your hearing."

The accounts of Mark and Matthew are somewhat different, yet the two show remarkable agreement. After John had been arrested, Mark tells us, "Jesus came to Galilee proclaiming the gospel of God: 'This is the time of fulfillment. The kingdom of God is at hand. Repent, and believe in the gospel'" (Mark 1:14-15). Matthew, too, tells us that John had been arrested and that Jesus had withdrawn to Galilee. Matthew takes the occasion to reinforce a text from the Hebrew Scriptures, showing Jesus as the fulfillment of that text:

Land of Zebulun and Naphthali, the way to the sea, beyond the Jordan, Galilee of the Gentiles, the people who sit in darkness have seen a great light, on those dwelling in a land overshadowed by death light has arisen.   (Matthew 4:15-16)

Matthew continues by saying that from that time on Jesus began to preach and say, "Repent, for the kingdom of heaven is at hand."

In Mark and Matthew and Luke, then, there is no question that a new phase in the life of Jesus has begun; but while Luke has permitted the reader to see this through the text of the prophet Isaiah, both Mark and Matthew announce the new day in a somewhat cryptic phrase: "The kingdom of heaven is at hand." Matthew's reference to Zebulun and Naphtali reminds us that two of Jacob's sons bore those names and that the names now refer (in Matthew's Gospel) to two of Israel's tribes. During the conquest of the Promised Land under Joshua, both tribes received portions of the land, as did the other tribes. The portion assigned to Zebulun is described in the nineteenth chapter of the Book of Joshua, beginning with the words, "The third lot fell to the clans of the Zebulunites." Naphtali's portion, too, is described in the same chapter, opening with the words, "The sixth lot fell to the Naphtalites." The text quoted by Matthew, however, derives from the prophecy of Isaiah, and Matthew finds its fulfillment in the Person of Jesus, the brightest of all lights. When the Assyrians began their invasion of the northern kingdom of Israel in the eighth century B.C.E., the first territories to be devastated were Zebulun and Naphtali. The northern capital of Samaria fell to the Assyrians in 721 B.C.E., and it is likely that the two tribes spoken of by Isaiah and now recalled by Matthew, felt the heel of the invader at an early date.

Indeed, when we look at the text of Isaiah to which Matthew refers, we find the prophet saying that the land of Zebulun and the land of Naphthali were degraded first: "But in the end he has glorified the seaward road, the land west of Jordan, the District of the Gentiles."

> Anguish has taken wing, dispelled in darkness:
>> for there is no gloom
>> where but now there was distress.
> The people who walked in darkness
>> have seen a great light;
> Upon those who dwelt in the land of gloom
>> a light has shone.
> You have brought them abundant joy
>> and great rejoicing,
> As they rejoice before you as at the harvest,
>> as men make merry when dividing spoils.
>
>> (Isaiah 8:23-9:2)

What we have seen thus far, then, is a certain similarity in the approach taken by Mark, Matthew and Luke, with Mark quoting simply the formula that reminds us of the preaching of John the Baptist, "Reform your lives; the kingdom of heaven is at hand." While Matthew and Luke quote the Hebrew Scriptures at this juncture in the life of Jesus, employing different texts, it is noteworthy that both quote from the prophecy of Isaiah: Matthew from early Isaiah (chapters 8 and 9), and Luke from the latter part of the prophecy (chapter 61). Matthew's text emphasizes light, the light that is Jesus incarnate; Luke's text stresses the bringing of glad tidings and liberty, armed as Jesus is with the spirit of the Lord God with which he is anointed.

It will seem a radical shift in scriptural texts to turn now to the Book of Nehemiah, a writing concerned with the rebuilding of the walls around the city of Jerusalem. Recall that when the armies of King Nebuchadnezzar of Babylon came to Jerusalem in 587 B.C.E. and conquered the city, carrying off hundreds of Jerusalem's inhabitants, the temple of Solomon was badly damaged and the walls surrounding the city were torn down in many places. At a much later date, a man named Nehemiah, employed in the imperial court of Persia, learned through messages that came to him about the pitiful condition of his beloved Jerusalem. A cupbearer in the Persian court, he requested King Artaxerxes that he be permitted to return for a while to the damaged city, to rebuild the walls that surrounded Jerusalem. The king permitted Nehemiah to take others with him and granted him letters for his safe travel. Returning to Jerusalem, Nehemiah found the walls indeed a shambles, but he set to work quickly, aided by his companions. Before long objections were raised: Sanballat, the governor of Samaria, opposed the rebuilding of the walls, and Sanballat was strengthened in his opposition by governors of neighboring provinces. Nehemiah nevertheless remained resolute, saying to those who assisted him:

> Our work is scattered and extensive, and we are widely separated from one another along the wall; wherever you hear the trumpet sound, join us there; our God will fight with us. (Nehemiah 4:13-14)

Elsewhere he wrote that it was "one arm to build with and one arm ever on one's sword."

Nehemiah lived several centuries before the time of the incarnate Lord Jesus, and his efforts in rebuilding the walls of Jerusalem well anticipate the scene that Jesus would enter upon at the time of his incarnation. That is to say, Jesus would experience a paucity of numbers willing to help, accompanied at times by strident opposition as he tried to build. It was not a wall, of course, that Jesus endeavored to build, but a kingdom: "Reform your lives; the kingdom of heaven is at hand."

Jesus stands in the center of human history, and Nehemiah anticipates the One who was to come. But the story does not end there. On the other side of the triptych, if we so wish to envision the scene, stand ourselves, hearkening to the word of our Savior and endeavoring with him to ready ourselves and the society about us for the kingdom that is at hand. On many sides are those who would oppose the rebuilding of the wall, who would contend that the wall — the kingdom — ought not be rebuilt. The kingdom of God began in the Garden of Eden with our first parents; but it was badly damaged by the fall of Adam and Eve, and despite God's efforts over and again throughout salvation history, opposition in one form or another keeps trying to prevent the rebuilding of the kingdom.

The incarnation of the Lord Jesus was the Father's way of calling all his children to repentance: all, after all, have been made in God's image and likeness. Recall the parable of Jesus concerning the king who sent many servants (God's prophets) and who finally sent his son. That Son is now with us, and with him came the kingdom of heaven of which Jesus speaks. The walls need rebuilding, and we, the builders, cannot afford to become discouraged by the opposition that now and then faces us. As with Nehemiah, we need to keep our hand on our sword — prayer, sacraments, all those helps provided for us through God's mercy. At the sound of the trumpet — the call of the community — we must come together to be further strengthened; then we must return to our rebuilding, confident that the great Light of whom Isaiah and Matthew speak, stands in our midst. Confident, too, that he who is God's anointed ("The Spirit of the Lord is upon me") has anointed us also, so that what we do is done not by our own strength, but through the power given us from above. "I am with you always."

18

GO TO SILOAM AND WASH

Perhaps no writer in the entire Bible has set forth so well the contrast between spiritual and physical blindness as has the writer of the fourth gospel. Long before reaching the ninth chapter of that book, we have grown accustomed to "signs." Of the changing of water into wine at the marriage feast at Cana the author has written: "Jesus did this as the beginning of his signs in Cana in Galilee and so revealed his glory, and his disciples began to believe in him" (John 2:11). Later, when a royal official hears that Jesus has returned to Galilee from Judea, he appeals to our Savior to come down and cure his son, near to death. At the words of the royal official, "Sir, come down before my child dies," Jesus responds, "You may go; your son will live." While on his way home the official is met by his slaves who tell him that the boy has recovered. Asked at what hour the boy had begun to recover, the slaves answer, "Yesterday, at about one in the afternoon," the very hour in which Jesus had said, "Your son will live." The father and his entire household came to believe. John writes: "This was the second sign Jesus did when he came to Galilee from Judea" (John 4:54).

There is subsequently a cure on the sabbath, and later Jesus is seen to walk on the water. While the word "sign" is not used in connection with these events, it is easy to see them as further signs of an extraordinary Presence in the world.

The ninth chapter of John's gospel is unique in many ways. Its very opening tells us that as Jesus passed by "he saw a man blind from birth" (John 9:1). No reference is made to the blind man asking for relief from his blindness; rather, the appearance of the blind man arouses a discussion, begun by the disciples of Jesus: "Rabbi, who sinned, this man or his parents, that he was born blind?" We almost feel ourselves back in the Book of Job, with the whole questions of physical evil again being debated: What had Job done? Here the question is, Has this man sinned, or his parents? Whose fault is this? Jesus is quick to respond, "Neither he nor his parents sinned; it is so that the works of God might be made visible through him" (John 9:3). We do not want to overlook a single word: "visible through him" means just what it says, for it will be through the blind man that some will come to see.

Jesus spits on the ground, we are told, and then he makes clay with the saliva and smears it on the blind man's eyes, bidding him go and wash in the pool of Siloam, "which means Sent," adds John. So the blind man went and washed, and came back able to see. It is precisely here that the drama begins. Those who had known the blind man as a beggar began to dispute about him, some contending that this was indeed the man who used to sit and beg, others insisting that he resembled that man, but was really someone else. John here inserts a tiny sentence uttered by the man born blind in response to a question directed to him to ascertain whether or not he really was the man born blind: "He said, 'I am'" (John 9:9). Further argument ensues, people doubting that this really could be the man born blind. They insist on an explanation, which he gives in ever so simple terms: "The man called Jesus made clay and anointed my eyes and told me, 'Go to Siloam and wash.' So I went there and washed and was able to see." When asked about the whereabouts of Jesus, the man replied, "I don't know."

The discussion has now reached such a pitch that those surrounding the man born blind bring him to the Pharisees. For the first time we are made aware that the event had taken place on a sabbath, and from earlier reading in John's Gospel we realize that this spells trouble for Jesus. Almost the same performance that we had seen earlier with the man born blind is now repeated for the Pharisees, who of course asked how he was able to see. The same reply is forthcoming: "He put clay on my eyes, and I washed, and now I can see." The very next sentence in the account helps us see that, in a sense, the axe has fallen, for there is an immediate decision on the part of the Pharisees: "This man is not from God, for he does not keep the sabbath" (John 9:16).

We cannot help noticing the artistry exercised by John as he develops the relationship (or the contrast) between spiritual and physical blindness. The Pharisees are well able to see; yet a prejudgment is passed, not because of any physical debility on their part, but simply because their hearts will not permit them to accept this one further sign in Jesus' ministry. "This man is not from God!" And why is he not from God? Because he does not (in their eyes) keep the sabbath.

Pharisees in the time of Jesus were, as a class, praiseworthy people who strove meticulously to observe the Mosaic Law, sacred to the Jews. That Law insisted on the keeping of the sabbath, and failure to do so all but branded a person as disrespectful of the Sinaitic covenant, the pact enacted by God with his people during the course of their travels in the wilderness, en route to the Land of Promise. The sabbath law, however, did not forbid the doing of good, as Jesus is at pains elsewhere in the gospel to point out. Recall the retort of the Master on another occasion: "If your ox or your ass falls into a pit on the sabbath, will you not pull him out?" If we may perform that kind of action on the sabbath, may we not in good faith heal another?

Not all the bystanders, of course, are willing to accept the claim of the Pharisees that Jesus is not from God: "How can a sinful man," they queried, "do such signs?" John here permits us to see light shining through the darkness: simple people recognize a Godly sign, while those best versed in the Law are unable to see clearly. Because there is division among the spectators, the man born blind is asked, "What do you have to say about him, since he opened your eyes?" Again an abundantly simple answer is forthcoming: "He is a prophet."

The man's parents are now called for, and we cannot help feeling that the darkness is deepening: how difficult for some to see clearly! The parents are fearful of the Pharisees and are willing to say only that the man was indeed born blind. And lest they be expelled from the synagogue for saying this, they add: "We do not know how he sees now, nor do we know who opened his eyes. Ask him, he is of age, he can speak for himself." We can almost hear their retort: "Ask *him!* Don't involve *us!*" Where do they stand in the darkness-sight situation? Are they seeing clearly? Or does threat, does fear tend to darken their vision?

The man born blind is again called for and questioned: "Give God the praise!" insist the questioners, completely unaware that that is precisely who ought to be getting the praise for the sign that has been accomplished! "Give God the praise! We know that this man is a sinner." "If he is a sinner," replied the man born blind, "I do not know. One thing I do know is that I was blind and now I see." But this will not do for his questioners: "What did he do to you? How did he open your eyes?" He answered them, "I told you already and you did not listen. Why do you want to hear it again?

Do you want to become his disciples, too?" Here we are aware that the man born blind is himself prophetic, himself a witness — not because of learned profundity, but simply because he is narrating the truth concerning Jesus and himself.

By this juncture the man born blind is understandably over-wrought, prompting him to reply to the persistence of his questioners with increasing vehemence. When they tell him that they do not know where Jesus is from, he retorts: "This is what is so amazing, that you do not know where he is from, yet he opened my eyes. We know that God does not listen to sinners, but if one is devout and does his will, he listens to him. It is unheard of that anyone ever opened the eyes of a person born blind. If this man were not from God, he would not be able to do anything" (John 9:30-33). Some readers of this passage have taken issue with the man's statement that God does not listen to sinners; but we must keep in mind that the man born blind is not a theologian. Rather, he is a simple man giving extraordinary witness to the Person of Jesus.

The argument becomes so heated and the man's adversaries so angry that ultimately they expel him. When Jesus hears of this he comes to the man and asks, "Do you believe in the Son of Man?" The man answers: "Who is he, sir, that I may believe in him?" "The one speaking with you is he," says Jesus. "I do believe," responds the man, and he worships Jesus.

The narrative concludes with our Savior leaving no doubt in the minds of the Pharisees about genuine sight and blindness. Continuing his conversation with the man born blind, Jesus says that he has come into the world that those who do not see might see, and that those who see might become blind. At that juncture the Pharisees object: "Surely we are not also blind, are we?" This gives Jesus the opportunity to say to them that if they were blind, they would have no sin. But because they keep insisting that they see, when in reality they are spiritually blind, their sin perdures.

Throughout the ninth chapter of John's Gospel we can hardly help coming back to the self: do I really see, or is my vision faulty because of my hardness of heart? What begins as a simple story of a man born blind becomes an examination of conscience for each of us.

19

UNEXHAUSTED FAVORS

f we carefully read the Book of Genesis we quickly become aware that the early chapters contain not one, but two accounts of creation. The first, which begins with a verse well known to all, "in the beginning," really concludes not with the end of the book's first chapter, but with the first part of the fourth verse of the second chapter. Then a second account gets underway, "At the time when the Lord God made the earth and the heavens...."

In creating humanity on the sixth day (in the first creation account), God says to his human creatures: "See, I give you every seed-bearing plant all over the earth and every tree that has seed-bearing fruit on it to be your food" (Genesis 1:29). Having created the earth, God now seems to be giving that earth over to his human creatures. In the second creation account, the sacred writer speaks of a garden: "Then the Lord God planted a garden in Eden, in the east, and he placed there the man whom he had formed" (Genesis 2:8). The garden has various trees delightful to look at and good for food, and a river that rises in Eden to water the garden divides into four branches, providing ample water for Eden and its inhabitants. Animals are formed by the Lord God, and toward the latter part of the second creation account Eve is formed from the rib of Adam. At the conclusion of the second chapter of Genesis, the garden created by the Lord God seem entirely idyllic.

A very different garden is presented to the reader of the New Testament who arrives at the Passion accounts in Mark, Matthew and Luke. Let us pause briefly to hear what each evangelist has to say.

At the Lord's Supper, writes Mark, Jesus foretold Peter's denial. But Peter vehemently replied: "'Even though I should have to die with you, I will not deny you.' And they all spoke similarly" (Mark 14:31). With those words ringing in our ears, we come at once to the garden. "Then they came to a place named Gethsemane, and he said to his disciples: 'Sit here while I pray.' He took with him Peter, James and John, and began to be troubled and distressed. Then he said to them, 'My soul is sorrowful even to death. Remain here and keep watch.' He advanced a little and fell to the ground and prayed that if it were possible the hour might pass by him; he said, 'Abba, Father, all things are possible to you. Take this cup away from me, but not what I will but what you will'" (Mark 14:32-36).

Students of the Scriptures have noted that Mark is not especially kind to the apostles: three separate times Jesus returns to the apostles, only to find them asleep. On the last occasion, our Savior says: "Are you still sleeping and taking your rest? It is enough. The hour has come. Behold, the Son of Man is to be handed over to sinners. Get up, let us go. See, my betrayer is at hand" (Mark 14:41-42).

Matthew's account of Peter's vehement statement about not denying Jesus is almost identical with that of Mark. He adds, as did Mark, "And all the disciples spoke likewise." Like Mark, also,

Matthew shows us Jesus coming to the garden at once. "Then Jesus came with them to a place called Gethsemane, and he said to his disciples, 'Sit here while I go over there and pray.' He took along Peter and the two sons of Zebedee, and began to feel sorrow and distress. Then he said to them, 'My soul is sorrowful even to death. Remain here and keep watch with me.' He advanced a little and fell prostrate in prayer, saying, 'My Father, if it is possible, let this cup pass from me; yet, not as I will, but as you will'" (Matthew 26:36-38).

What follows closely resembles Mark: three times our Savior goes off to pray, and on each return the disciples are asleep. On the third occasion Matthew writes pretty much as does Mark: "Are you still sleeping and taking your rest? Behold the hour is at hand when the Son of Man is to be handed over to sinners. Get up, let us go. Look, my betrayer is at hand" (Matthew 26:45-46).

In the Gospel of Luke, Peter's denial of Jesus is foretold by our Savior, but the third evangelist quotes Peter as replying, "Lord, I am prepared to go to prison and to die with you" (Luke 22:33). Luke here inserts further words of Jesus concerning a time of crisis unique to the Gospel accounts.

He said to them, "When I sent you forth without a money bag or a sack or sandals, were you in need of anything?" "No, nothing," they replied. He said to them, "But now one who has a money bag should take it, and likewise a sack, and one who does not have a sword should sell his cloak and buy one. For I tell you that this scripture must be fulfilled in me, namely, 'He was counted among the wicked'; and indeed, what is written about me is coming to fulfillment." Then they said, "Lord, look, there are two swords here." But he replied, "It is enough" (Luke 22:35-38).

Luke then continues his account by showing Jesus and the

disciples going out. "He went, as was his custom, to the Mount of Olives, and the disciples followed him. When he arrived at the place he said to them, 'Pray that you may not undergo the test.' After withdrawing about a stone's throw from them and kneeling, he prayed, saying, 'Father, if you are willing, take this cup away from me; still, not my will but yours be done.' And to strengthen him an angel from heaven appeared to him. He was in such agony and he prayed so fervently that his sweat became like drops of blood falling on the ground" (Luke 22:39-44).

The threefold return of Jesus to the sleeping disciples is absent in Luke's Gospel. There is but one return, and even that is softened by the evangelist as he writes: "When he rose from prayer and returned to his disciples, he found them sleeping from grief. He said to them: 'Why are you sleeping? Get up and pray that you may not undergo the test'" (Luke 22:45-46).

The three Gospel writers now portray the betrayal by Judas, an account with which we are all quite familiar. Details differ from writer to writer, but the essence of the account tells us that Jesus is betrayed by one of the Twelve, emphasized over and again in the New Testament, perhaps as a reminder to each of us that discipleship is not a guarantee of steadfastness, apart from God's loving grace.

The contrast between the garden known as Eden and the garden known as Gethsemane may seem at first sight so great that little room is left for comparison. But we cannot afford to move to conclusions too quickly. Eden was indeed exactly that: a paradise designed for the human race. The sin that entered Eden, however, in the fall of our first parents, gave a new slant to humanity's history, and Gethsemane must be seen in the light of that fall. Not everyone interprets the words of the Lord God to the serpent (Genesis 3:15) in the same way: "I will put enmity between you and the woman, and between your offspring and hers; he will strike at your head, while you strike at his heel." We may see here nevertheless the first promise of a Redeemer for fallen humankind. If we so view that text, the relation between Eden and Gethsemane appears not so far apart: the garden in which Jesus prays for the cup to pass signals the beginning of the triumph of the Savior, a triumph that has been preceded by bitter moments indeed, but moments that were always in harmony with the Father's will. Perhaps Luke's account comes closest to reality when he writes that the sweat of Jesus becomes as drops of blood, so intense the passion of him who would effect our salvation.

"The favors of the Lord are not exhausted, his mercies are not spent. They are renewed each morning, so great is his faithfulness" (Lamentations 22-23). While it is commonly believed that the Book of Lamentations was written in the light of the Babylonian Exile (587 B.C.E.), when great numbers of Jerusalem's people were carried off to Babylon by the armies of Nebuchadnezzar, it is surely not accidental that the Church, particularly during her Holy Week liturgy, goes back time and again to that book in contemplating the sufferings and death of the Lord Jesus. "Come, all you who pass by the way, look and see whether there is any suffering like my suffering" (Lamentations 1:12). Verses are culled over and again to reflect the bitterness of the gall drunk by our Savior in his Passion. At the same time, we want to see in Lamentations the confidence of Jesus in his Father, the realization that the favors of the Lord are not exhausted. He who is the Word of God, he who abode in the bosom of the Trinity from the beginning, knows the Father, and in that knowing is aware that God's mercies are renewed each morning, so great is his faithfulness.

Have our lives about them that same confidence, particularly as we confront life's difficulties? Are our hearts lifted up, so that we can see in our present suffering the resurrection that must follow, as night the day? For the believing Christian, Holy Week can never be simply a concentration on the sufferings of Jesus Christ; so to think would be to betray again the Redeemer of the world. No, the favors of the Lord are not exhausted, his mercies are not spent.

20

TO WALK WITH JESUS

Not surprisingly, those who travel to Israel are often anxious to visit one or the other site sacred to them for religious reasons. The city of Jerusalem is considered a very special place not only by Israelis, but by Moslems and Christians as well. For many centuries now, Christians have been able to pursue the way of the cross, the path taken by Jesus on his way to Calvary's hill, a way that today wanders through various streets en route to the place of Jesus' crucifixion.

Each of the four evangelists found in the New Testament of the Bible has devoted two chapters near the latter part of his Gospel to what are often spoken of as the Passion Narratives. In great detail, at times, these narratives describe the events that (in some instances) began with Jesus in Gethsemane, and continue on through the trial scenes to the crucifixion and death of Jesus. Several of the events spoken of in the Passion Narratives eventually found their way into a devotion that soon became popular throughout much of the Catholic world, the Stations of the Cross. Those who developed the devotion, however, interspersed with the biblical scenes other aspects of the suffering Jesus, leading eventually to a series of fourteen stations that combine non-scriptural events with scenes taken from the Passion Narratives.

Of late there has been some movement to add a fifteenth station, namely, the resurrection of Jesus, in order that the devotion will conclude on a positive note. In 1991, a handsome book, *The Reversible Dream*, written and illustrated by Elizabeth Augenblick, was published. It contained two sets of stations: Stations of Sorrow and Stations of Joy, each beautifully illustrated and accompanied by an appropriate text. Catholic theology clearly teaches that the crucifixion is not to be seen in isolation, but always in relation to the triumph that followed on the third day, the resurrection of Jesus from the tomb. Not everyone sees the addition of a fifteenth station as being desirable; but here and there, in making the Stations of the Cross, you come upon a church or chapel in which a fifteenth station been added to the customary fourteen. In some places, too, a new arrangement of the traditional fourteen stations has been inaugurated, eliminating stations that are non-scriptural, and substituting events clearly recorded in the Passion Narratives.

The traditional fourteen stations begin with an incredible irony: man is judging God! For a time Pilate seems to be trying to release Jesus, but when he hears the cry, "If you release him, you are no friend of Caesar!", he capitulates and gives Jesus over to be crucified. For the Roman soldiers, the process is now routine: scourging, imposition of the crossbeam of the cross, and the driving of the victim along to the place of crucifixion. But the stations do not detail all of these actions; rather, they move quickly to show the soldiers imposing the wood of the cross on him who is to be crucified.

Before the devotion now known as the Stations of the Cross came to be formalized, tradition had it that our Savior fell from time to time on the way to Calvary under the burden of the cross.

Sacred Scripture is silent about this, but so strong was the tradition that three stations — the third, the seventh and the ninth — are graphic reminders of the burden attached to the journey of Jesus.

When the angel Gabriel appeared to Mary (according to the Gospel of Saint Luke), the opening salutation of Gabriel was, "Hail, favored one! The Lord is with you." More than three decades have now passed, and as Jesus moves along the sorrowful way to the hill of crucifixion, tradition has it that he encountered his mother. How distant then must have sounded the voice of Gabriel; yet we, contemplating mother and divine Son, can echo the words of the angel, "Hail, favored one! The Lord is with you!" Jesus is still Lord, however bedraggled he may appear to the bystanders; and although his mother may have but a fleeting moment in which to speak with him, surely the Lord is with her.

Saint Luke tells his readers that "as they led Jesus away they took hold of a certain Simon, a Cyrenian, who was coming in from the country; and after laying the cross on him, they made him carry it behind Jesus" (Luke 23:26). The Gospel accounts of both Mark and Matthew, too, make mention of Simon, and of his being pressed into service to assist Jesus. It is this scene that serves as the fifth station. Books of meditation on the stations frequently make reference to the willingness, or its lack, of the individual Christian to help Jesus in his hour of great need.

A non-scriptural station follows, as Veronica wipes the face of Jesus. It is worth noting that the name Veronica means "true image," and it is perhaps the long tradition attaching to the story of this valiant woman that has given her her name. As our Savior trudges along on his way to Calvary, a woman, undaunted by the crowd and the animosity of those who wished Jesus crucified, approaches Jesus and proffers a towel. He wipes his face with the towel and returns it to this kind and caring woman, leaving the impression of his countenance on the towel. Although the story is non-scriptural and despite the fact that some will not want to trust the tradition attaching to the story, it is perhaps one of the "truest" stories one can imagine, for in ministering to the suffering, we ourselves receive an ever greater image of Christ Jesus in our own being.

Between the sixth and eighth stations we encounter the second fall of Jesus, yet despite the suffering involved in each fall, we find our Savior, in the eighth station, stopping to speak to the women of Jerusalem. Only in the Gospel of Luke is this scene described: "A large crowd of people followed Jesus, including many women who mourned and lamented him. Jesus turned to them and said, 'Daughters of Jerusalem, do not weep for me; weep instead for yourselves and your children'" (Luke 23:27-28). The text of Luke is important in several ways, and not least of all because it permits us to see that not all of the spectators of Jesus' passion were inimical to him. Indeed, the language employed by the evangelist makes us feel that the "many women" spoken of were aggrieved at what they beheld. As we read this part of Luke, we are reminded that in the long history of monastic prayer, the gift of tears was consistently seen as a genuine indication of one's desire for true conversion of life.

The tenth station, which follows upon the third fall of Jesus, speaks of our Savior being stripped of his garments. The Gospel of Luke makes no mention of a stripping, but the other three evangelists carry accounts of it. Was it to this stripping that the tenth station refers, or was the station intended to remind us that prior to the nailing to the cross and the crucifixion, Jesus was first stripped of his garments? In the Gospel passages that speak of an earlier stripping, the latter forms part of the trial scene. Matthew writes: "Then the soldiers of the governor took Jesus inside the praetorium and gathered the whole cohort around him. They stripped off his clothes and threw a scarlet military cloak about him" (Matthew 27:27-28). Mark and John do not mention stripping directly, but each indicates that Jesus was scourged in the course of the trial, intimating certainly that his garments had been stripped from him. "So Pilate, wishing to satisfy the crowd, released Barabbas to them, and, after he had Jesus scourged, handed him over to be crucified. The soldiers led him away inside the palace, that is, the praetorium, and assembled the whole cohort. They clothed him in purple and, weaving a crown of thorns, placed it on him" (Mark 15:15-17). John's handling is similar, though a bit briefer: "Then Pilate took Jesus and had him scourged. And the soldiers wove a crown out of thorns and placed it on his head, and clothed him in a purple cloak" (John 19:1-2).

In many churches in which the stations of the cross have been erected, the eleventh station often bears the inscription, "Jesus is nailed to the cross." None of the evangelists mentions a nailing: all say, quite simply, they crucified him, without making mention of the way in which the crucifixion was carried out. In the course of the centuries, however, devotion to the nails grew, and today we all but take for granted that nails pierced the hands and feet of Jesus. It would seem that when the evangelists wrote, readers were well aware of what went on in the process of crucifixion, and there was little need to say anything beyond this: viz., that they crucified him.

The four evangelists write differently concerning the death of Jesus on the cross, the twelfth station. "Jesus gave a loud cry," writes Mark, "and breathed his last" (Mark 15:37). Matthew writes: "But Jesus cried out again in a loud voice and gave up his spirit" (Matthew 27:50). Luke's Gospel reads: "Jesus cried out in a loud voice, 'Father, into your hands I commend my spirit'; and when he had said this he breathed his last" (Luke 23:46). John, finally, writes: "When Jesus had taken the wine, he said, 'It is finished.' And bowing his head, he handed over the spirit" (John 19:30).

Tradition has added an element in the thirteenth station that is not found in the Scriptures. While all of the evangelists recount the removal of the body of Jesus from the cross, none makes mention of his being entrusted to the arms of his mother. But from an early date Christian piety saw this as a fitting ending, just prior to our Savior's body being placed in the sepulchre, the fourteenth station. Coupled with the tradition of Jesus' being given over to his mother there exist books of devotion that suggest that for every Christian, it is most fitting to pray at the thirteenth station that we, too, might be entrusted to the care of our Lady at the hour of our death, echoing the final petition of the Hail Mary: Pray for us sinners now and at the hour of our death.

Devotional books, commenting on the fourteenth station, sometimes mention the impossibility for the tomb to contain the body of the dead Jesus: surely his rising will burst the bonds of death. More recent piety, as mentioned earlier, sometimes inclines to a fifteenth station, so that the non-finality of death may be made abundantly clear to Christian piety.

However we make the Stations of the Cross, as the expression goes, we cannot help but recognize the enormous love of the Savior of mankind for his people: who would undergo suffering such as that encountered by Jesus if he had not a deep and abiding love for those created in the image and likeness of the Father? How great a privilege, then, for each of us to be able to walk with Jesus!

21

WORDS FROM THE CROSS

mong the writers of the Gospel, it is only the fourth evangelist who introduces his work with a prologue that situates the Son of God in the bosom of the Trinity for all eternity: "In the beginning was the Word, and the Word was with God, and the Word was God" (John 1:1). Several verses later John writes: "And the Word became flesh and made his dwelling among us, and we saw his glory, the glory as of the Father's only Son, full of grace and truth" (John 1:14). Then the evangelist moves to the testimony given by John the Baptist: "This was he of whom I said, 'The one who is coming after me ranks ahead of me because he existed before me.'"

After the Baptist has given testimony concerning himself, he gives testimony to the Lord Jesus, and when Jesus walked by, John said to the two disciples accompanying him, "Behold, the Lamb of God." Before the first chapter of John's Gospel has concluded Jesus has chosen as disciples Andrew and his brother Simon Peter, Philip, and Nathanael. The second chapter of John opens with the evangelist telling us that on the third day there was a wedding in Cana in Galilee and that the mother of Jesus was there. The use of the expression, "the third day," in the Hebrew Scriptures has been noted elsewhere, and it is worthwhile observing its appearance here and in other places in the New Testament as well. When the wine has run short and the mother of Jesus calls his attention to this, Jesus says to her, "Woman, how does your concern affect me? My hour has not yet come" (John 2:4).

"The agony (in the Garden)," writes Father Raymond Brown, "is the chief place in the Synoptic Gospels that we hear Jesus use the term 'hour' for the passion…. The use of hour is found over ten times in John to describe the whole complexus of the passion and elevation of Jesus, and its spiritual effects" (Raymond E. Brown, *New Testament Essays*, page 195). When Jesus employs the word hour in speaking at Cana to his mother, some believe that the evangelist John is deliberately relating this early phase of Mary's life in the public life of Jesus to the "raising up" in chapter 19 of John's Gospel, where we read: "Standing by the cross of Jesus were his mother and his mother's sister, Mary the wife of Clopas, and Mary of Magdala. When Jesus saw his mother and the disciple there whom he loved, he said to his mother, 'Behold, your son.' Then he said to the disciple, 'Behold, your mother.' And from that *hour* the disciple took her into his home" (John 19:25-27). Understandably, whether or not the Cana scene is related to this part of the Gospel of John, the words of Jesus, hanging on the cross, are seen as part of the body of sayings attributed to his final hours.

In the course of the centuries following upon the crucifixion and resurrection of Jesus, Christian piety has reflected on the words uttered by Jesus on the cross, and today there continues to be a very genuine devotion to what are sometimes called the Seven Last Words of Christ. Composers have set the words to music, and those responsible for such compositions have endeavored to match their musical expressions with the sense of the impassioned words.

The Passion accounts of the four evangelists differ one from another, yet, at the same time, there are similarities. Only in the Gospel of Mark does Jesus pray that the *hour* might pass him by; but in both Mark and Matthew reference is made to the *hour* at hand. "Are you still sleeping and taking your rest? It is enough. The *hour* has come. Behold, the Son of Man is to be handed over to sinners" (Mark 14:41); "then he returned to his disciples and said to them, 'Are you still sleeping and taking your rest? Behold, the *hour* is at hand when the Son of Man is to be handed over to sinners'" (Matthew 26:45).

The words that are to be uttered in Jesus' *hour* differ from one evangelist to another. Only Mark and Matthew have almost identical words, the first verse of Psalm 22, thought by some to have been recited by our Savior on the cross. Mark reads: "Eloi, Eloi, lema sabachthani, my God, my God, why have you forsaken me?" (Mark 15:34). Apart from Mark's use of Aramaic (Eloi, Eloi), Matthew's words are identical: "Eli, Eli, lema sabachthani, my God, my God, why have you forsaken me?" (Matthew 27:46). In the listing of the seven last words of Jesus in popular devotion and in musical settings, this quotation from Psalm 22 is seen as the fourth of our Savior's words.

The remaining six words are divided evenly between the passion narratives of Luke and John. Significantly, Jesus' words of forgiveness uttered from the cross, "Father, forgive them, they know not what they do," the first word uttered on the cross by Jesus, are found in the Gospel of Luke 23:34. Homilists and ministers of the word have often made much of the position of this word among the final words of Jesus, seeing it to be in complete harmony with the ministry of our Savior throughout his public life. The second word, too, spoken by Jesus to the thief hanging to his right, are similarly seen as characteristic of a Savior who sacrificed his life that sinners might live: "Amen, I say to you, today you will be with me in Paradise" (Luke 23:43).

The third word ("Woman, behold your son; son, behold your mother"), briefly referred to above, is addressed, as noted there, to the mother of Jesus and the beloved disciple. Some see in Jesus' words at Cana ("My hour has not yet come") an invitation to his mother to join her *hour* to his, and they find the fulfillment of that in the third word, found only in the passion narrative of John. The third word on the cross has been given still further interpretations, however, for Mary is seen as mother of the Church, represented at the foot of the cross in the person of the beloved disciple, faithful to the suffering Jesus to the very end.

"All men live to die," writes Father Paschal Botz. "Christians die to live." The author is commenting on Psalm 22, and continues as follows:

> They find God in suffering. The silence of God in suffering is the way of faith. Solitude and abandonment are themes of this Psalm. The hardest trial of suffering for believers is the feeling of abandonment by God, the God who has taken such good care of us from our mother's womb, the God of our happy youth, the God who answered our prayers. Sick unto death, his body wasting away, with nothing to look forward to, surrounded by enemies like hungry lions and senseless dogs, the Psalmist reaches out with his last thread of strength to the Presence of God.
>
> (Paschal Botz, O.S.B., *Runways to God*, page 44)

It is this psalm which begins with the words, "My God, my

God, why have you forsaken me?" Some have found difficulties with these words on the lips of Jesus, asking how the Father could forsake his beloved Son. The text of this fourth word must be seen, of course, in its context: it is the beginning of a psalm expressing abandonment and, seen in its context, may well express the forsaken feelings that could have taken hold of the suffering Jesus on Calvary.

Only in the Gospel of John is the fifth word found: "I thirst" (John 19:28). The evangelist adds that there was a vessel filled with common wine: "So they put a sponge soaked in wine on a sprig of hyssop and put it up to his mouth" (John 19:29). Almost at once comes the sixth of the seven words, "It is finished." "And bowing his head," writes John, "he handed over the spirit" (John 19:30).

There remains but one word, and that is found only in the Gospel of Luke. It was now about noon, writes Luke, and darkness came over the whole land until three in the afternoon. These were the very hours during which lambs for the paschal meal were being slain, in all probability, for those celebrating Passover in Jerusalem. "Then the veil of the temple," writes Luke, "was torn down the middle."

Psalm 31 is a prayer to the Lord in a time of distress and, at the same time, moves us to offer thanksgiving for deliverance granted. The final word of Jesus on the cross, found in Luke's Gospel, seems to be a verse of that psalm: Luke's Gospel indicates that our Savior added one word, "Father," to the psalm verse, so that the seventh word reads: "Father, into your hands I commend my spirit" (Luke 23:46). The evangelist adds that, when Jesus had said this, he breathed his last.

We come to recognize why our forbears in the Faith found both solace and food for contemplation in the final words of Jesus as portrayed by the evangelists. There is nothing of bitterness, nothing of revenge, nothing of a failed mission: throughout the agony, as seen by the writers of the Gospel, those very things that Jesus did and taught were exemplified. On which of the words shall we concentrate our attention? The forgiveness of the first word? The promise of redemption in the second? The gift of the mother of Jesus to ourselves in the third? The awful feeling of desertion in the fourth? The parched feeling of non-love in the fifth? The realization of all being completed in the sixth? The comfort of finally "going home" in the seventh?

No; we shall want to meditate on all of the words, for each is a treasure bequeathed to us by the Son of Man. "Truly," said the centurion, "this was the Son of God."

22

ON THE THIRD DAY

In the Book of Hosea, in the sixth chapter, we read:

> In their affliction, they shall look for me:
> "Come, let us return to the Lord,
>   for it is he who has rent, but he will heal us:
>   he has struck us, but he will bind our wounds.
> He will revive us after two days,
>   on the third day he will raise us up,
>   to live in his presence." (Hosea 6:1-2)

In the Book of Genesis, the patriarch Joseph has been in prison for a crime of which he was not guilty. During his stay there he interpreted correctly the dreams of two of his fellow-prisoners. In each instance, that which was foretold by Joseph concerning the dreams was to take place within three days. We read, in the fortieth chapter of Genesis:

> And in fact, on the third day, which was Pharaoh's birthday, when he gave a banquet to all his staff, with his courtiers around him, he lifted up the heads of the chief cupbearer and chief baker. (Genesis 40:20)

Earlier in the Book of Genesis, when Abraham was asked by God to sacrifice his son Isaac, the two set out for the place of which God had told Abraham. "On the third day Abraham got sight of the place from afar" (Genesis 22:4).

The above instances are selected from many that might be cited in the Hebrew Scriptures, stressing the third day. While the precise meaning of the text may not always be abundantly clear, very often the expression indicates a turn of events for the better. We are not surprised, therefore, in coming to the resurrection accounts in the Gospel and learning there that Jesus rose on the third day. The evangelist John is faithful to this tradition when, at the beginning of the twentieth chapter, he writes: "On the first day of the week, Mary of Magdala came to the tomb early in the morning." Here "the first day of the week" (Sunday) is the third day after the crucifixion of Jesus, a day that will prove one of liberation not only for the crucified Savior, but also for the entire world that Jesus had come to redeem. Coming to the tomb, Mary discovered that the stone had been moved. She ran to tell Peter and the other disciple whom Jesus loved that the Lord had been taken from the tomb. Peter and the beloved disciple ran to the tomb, discovered things to be as Mary had described, and entered the tomb. The beloved disciple, writes John, "saw and believed." The evangelist goes on to say that "they did not yet understand the scripture that he had to rise from the dead. Then the disciples returned home" (John 20:9-10).

John's Resurrection Narrative differs here from those of Mark and Matthew and Luke (and they, in turn, differ from one another in several respects) in that only Mary Magdalene is mentioned. All of the other accounts give names of other women coming to the tomb with Mary of Magdala. While the latter weeps outside the tomb (in John's account), a stranger appears whom Mary mistakes for the gardener. He addresses to her the same question she had heard a bit earlier from two angels she encountered in the tomb, "Woman, why are you weeping?" In response to the "gardener's" question she responds: "Sir, if you carried him away, tell me where you laid him, and I will take him." Jesus then said to her, "Mary!" and she immediately recognizes him and says to him, "Rabbouni!" (my teacher). Jesus tells her that he has not yet ascended to the Father; she is to go to his brothers and say: "I am going to my Father and your Father, my God and your God."

Several observations ought be made here concerning the resurrection of Jesus. Foremost, perhaps, is this (mentioned in an earlier meditation), that Jesus has entered into a new reality, the risen life, the *eschaton* or end time, a form of being entirely different from the natural life in which Mary and the disciples had known him heretofore. The mention, too, of his having to ascend is also very important, for resurrection, ascension and the coming of the Holy Spirit need to be seen as part of an integral series of events. A book written prior to the Gospel of John, the Acts of the Apostles, begins with an account of Jesus' appearance prior to the ascension, and then goes on to speak of that event quite graphically before coming to recount the descent of the Holy Spirit. John, on the other hand, brings together the three mysteries in the twentieth chapter of his Gospel. Theologically, the Church from her early days emphasized that the Spirit could not come until Jesus had been glorified by the Father, that is, had ascended to the Father. As will be seen momentarily, John in his Gospel maintains the pattern of resurrection, ascension and sending of the Spirit, through the sequence of events narrated in his twentieth chapter.

For fear of the Jews, writes John, the disciples had locked

themselves in a room on "the evening of the first day of the week." Jesus came and stood in their midst and said to them, "Peace be with you. As the Father has sent me, so I send you." Breathing on them, he said, "Receive the Holy Spirit. Whose sins you forgive are forgiven them, and whose sins you retain are retained" (John 20:19-23). There next follows the account of the missing Thomas, the story of his doubt, the reappearance of Jesus a week later, and Thomas' profession of faith. Much has been made, and reasonably so, of the words used by Thomas, "My Lord and my God!" Pheme Perkins, in her commentary on John's Gospel in the *Jerome Biblical Commentary*, speaks of Thomas' expression as the culmination of the Gospel's christology, since it acknowledges the crucified/exalted Jesus as "Lord and God." Whatever confidence may have been lacking in the disciples concerning the divinity of Jesus is now overcome in the face of the reality of the Savior's resurrection.

Elsewhere it has been noted that each of the Gospel writers has devoted his final chapter to an account of the resurrection, excepting John, who devotes his two final chapters to stories concerning that event. Consideration has already been given the first of those chapters. The final chapter, sometimes spoken of as an epilogue, contains material peculiar to John, stories that help illumine the Gospel that began with "In the beginning was the Word."

Peter, the sons of Zebedee, and four other disciples are fishing as the chapter opens. At dawn, Jesus stands on the shore, but at first he is not recognized by the disciples. When Jesus is told that they have caught nothing, he bids them cast their net over the starboard side of the boat, and once they had done so they were not able to pull their net in because of the enormous catch. "It is the Lord," cried the beloved disciple to Peter. When the disciples arrived at the shore, Jesus invited them to breakfast with him.

Following the meal, Jesus addresses himself three times to

Peter, "Simon, son of John, do you love me more than these?" When Peter has responded each time in the affirmative, Jesus says to him:

> Amen, amen I say to you, when you were younger, you used to dress yourself and go where you wanted, but when you grow old, you will stretch out your hands, and someone else will dress you and lead you where you do not want to go. (John 21:18)

The evangelist then goes on to explain that Jesus thus signified the kind of death by which Peter would glorify God. Then Jesus says, "Follow me."

Again we will want to pause to ask what this text is saying in our own life. Each of us, when we are young, does indeed often run pretty much in the way we wish. But as time goes on and as the circumstances of life grow more complex, often we can no longer run at our own behest. If we accept the evangelist's interpretation, Peter's martyrdom is here being foretold by Jesus. In our own situations, it need not be martyrdom that faces us, yet there is a working out of *our* salvation that the events of life often enough effect. While the Sacred Scriptures tell us that God wills our holiness, Scripture does not tell us precisely how that holiness is to be worked out. The maturing years often shed light on the way in which an all-loving God fashions our sanctity.

When Peter turned around and saw the beloved disciple following, he raised a question with Jesus: "Lord, what about him?" Our Savior responds: "What if I want him to remain until I come? What concern is it of yours? You follow me." Twice now in a matter of a few moments we have heard Jesus say to Peter, "Follow me." Recall that it is to the pastor of the Church established by Jesus to whom our Savior is speaking. First Jesus had asked Peter whether he loved him, and that three times. Then he foretold the kind of death by which Peter would achieve salvation. Now he says to him not once, but twice, "Follow me."

What are the keys to our everlasting life? Surely, in the first place, a genuine love of the Savior. Accompanying that is an acceptance of what God has in store for us, the kind of path in which our lives will be walked. Finally, there is to be no looking back, but a constant remembrance of how Jesus invited the prince of the apostles to make his way heavenward: "Follow me, follow me!"

23

WOMAN, WHY ARE YOU WEEPING?

It is generally believed among students of the Sacred Scriptures that the author of Saint Mark's Gospel concluded his work with verse eight of the sixteenth chapter. The Gospel goes on, as readers of the New Testament are well aware, to verse 20 and is looked upon as part of the inspired Gospel; but it seems altogether possible that a hand other than that of Mark wrote verses 9-20.

Comparatively few persons appear in any lengthy treatment in all four Gospel accounts, and apart from the Mother of Jesus only one woman lays claim to that privilege — Mary Magdalene, who appears in both the Passion and Resurrection narratives in each Gospel. In the Gospel of Mark, for example, the final sentence in the Passion narrative reads: "Mary Magdalene and Mary the mother of Joses watched where he was laid" (Mark 15:47).

Mark begins his Resurrection account by telling the reader that "when the sabbath was over, Mary Magdalene, Mary the mother of James, and Salome bought spices so that they might go and anoint" Jesus. They had wondered who would roll back the stone from the tomb for them, but on arriving there they discovered that the stone had already been rolled back.

On entering the tomb they saw a young man sitting on the right side, clothed in a white robe, and they were utterly amazed. He said to them: "Do not be amazed! You seek Jesus of Nazareth, the crucified. He has been raised: he is not here. Behold, the place where they laid him. But go and tell his disciples and Peter, 'He is going before you to Galilee; there you will see him, as he told you.'" Then they went out and fled from the tomb, seized with trembling and bewilderment. They said nothing to anyone, for they were afraid. (Mark 16:58)

If someone were to ask why it is generally believed that a hand other than that of Mark wrote the verses following this account, a careful reading of what follows would give at least a clue to the answer. Verse 9 begins by telling us that when Jesus had risen, early on the first day of the week, "he appeared first to Mary Magdalene, out of whom he had driven seven demons. She went and told his companions who were mourning and weeping. When they heard that he was alive and had been seen by her, they did not believe" (Mark 16:9-11). We have, then, in these few verses from Mark two very different accounts: in one instance the women said nothing to anyone because they were afraid; in the second account Mary went and reported to Jesus' companions what she herself had witnessed.

In the Passion account found in Saint Matthew's Gospel, Joseph of Arimathea asked Pilate for the body of Jesus, and Pilate ordered it to be handed over. "Taking the body, Joseph wrapped it in clean linen and laid it in his new tomb that he had hewn in the rock. Then he rolled a huge stone across the entrance to the tomb and departed. But Mary Magdalene and the other Mary remained sitting there, facing the tomb" (Matthew 27:59-61).

You may recall that Matthew speaks of the earth quaking at the death of Jesus. Now, "after the sabbath, as the first day of the week was dawning, Mary Magdalene and the other Mary came to see the tomb. And behold, there was a great earthquake; for an angel of the Lord descended from heaven, approached, rolled back the stone, and sat upon it" (Matthew 28:1-2). The angel bade the women not to be afraid, invited the women to see the place where Jesus' body had lain, and told them to go quickly to tell the disciples that Jesus had been raised and was going before them to Galilee. "Then they went away quickly from the tomb, fearful yet overjoyed," writes Matthew, "and ran to announce this to his disciples. And behold, Jesus met them on their way and greeted them. They approached, embraced his feet, and did him homage. Then Jesus said to them, 'Do not be afraid. Go tell my brothers to go to Galilee, and there they will see me'" (Matthew 28:8-10).

The final two verses at Saint Luke's Passion Narrative, speaking of the burial of Jesus, inform us that "the women who had come from Galilee with him followed behind, and when they had seen the tomb and the way in which his body was laid in it, they returned and prepared spices and perfumed oils. Then they rested on the sabbath according to the commandment" (Luke 23:55-56).

Luke's Resurrection account hardly seems an interruption of what we have just read: "But at daybreak on the first day of the week they took the spices they had prepared and went to the tomb" (Luke 24:1). The stone was already rolled away, and the women entered the tomb only to find that the body of Jesus was not there. Two men in dazzling garments appeared and asked: "Why do you seek the living one among the dead? He is not here, he has been raised. Remember what he said to you while he was still in Galilee, that the Son of Man must be handed over to sinners and be crucified, and rise on the third day" (Luke 24:5-7). The women recalled the words, Luke tells us, and returned from the tomb and announced all these things to the eleven and to the others. Luke now tells us who the women were: Mary Magdalene, Joanna, and Mary the mother of James; "the others who accompanied them also told this to the apostles, but their story seemed like nonsense and they did not believe them" (Luke 24:10-11).

In his Passion account, John the evangelist tells us: "Standing by the cross of Jesus were his mother and his mother's sister, Mary, the wife of Clopas, and Mary of Magdala" (John 19:25). In beginning the Resurrection account John writes: "On the first day of the week, Mary of Magdala came to the tomb early in the morning, while it was still dark, and saw the stone removed from the tomb" (John 20:1). She ran to tell Simon Peter and the disciple whom Jesus loved. The evangelist John then tells us about Peter and the beloved disciple coming to the tomb and examining it. Mary, meanwhile, "stayed outside the tomb weeping." She saw inside the tomb two angels in white, and they said to her, "Woman, why are you weeping?" "They have taken my Lord," she answered, "and I don't know where they laid him" (John 20:11-13). It is then that Mary mistakes Jesus for the gardener, and he, too, addresses to her the same question already asked by the angels: "Woman, why are you weeping?" "Sir," says Mary, "if you carried him away, tell me where you laid him, and I will take him." Jesus then says to her, "Mary," and she recognizes her risen Lord (John 20:15-16). What follows is important to us, not least of all because it is through the words of the risen Jesus to Mary that she learns that he must still ascend to the Father.

> Jesus said to her, "Stop holding on to me, for I have not yet ascended to the Father. But go to my brothers and tell them, 'I am going to my Father and your Father, to

my God and your God.'" Mary of Magdala went and
announced to the disciples, "I have seen the Lord," and
what he told her.   (John 20:17-18)

All four of the Gospel accounts, therefore, manifest the closeness of Mary Magdalene to the Passion and Resurrection narratives.
We are already aware of differences in the reporting of the four
evangelists. Those differences are surely prominent in the final pages
of each Gospel. Yet each evangelist makes it clear that Mary of
Magdala (to use John's term) figures importantly in the closing
moments of Jesus' life as man and in his resurrection.

Of great importance to us as we read the Resurrection narratives is the realization that the Jesus confronted by Mary Magdalene
(and the other women) is and is not the same Jesus known to them
prior to the resurrection. It is indeed the same Jesus who had walked
the hills of Galilee and worshiped in the temple at Jerusalem; yet
it seems not to be the same Jesus because he had now entered into
an existence quite different from the mortal life he had known prior
to his death. None of the Gospel writers uses the theological terms
that are now part and parcel of our vocabulary; but through their
simple telling of the events surrounding the resurrection the Church
established by Jesus has come to understand the important distinc-
tion, for example, between ordinary human life (fraught with its
mortality) and eschatological life, that form of existence that is
without end.

When Mary and the other women beheld the risen Savior,
they were face to face with the eschatologized Jesus, the Jesus who
sits at the right hand of the Father and whose existence is without
end. In facing the risen Jesus, too, they were facing their own future — not one doomed to everlasting extinction, but a life in which

their bodies, too, would share the *eschaton*, the time without end, that is the everlasting kingdom of God.

"Woman, why are you weeping?" How often the same question is (or can be) addressed to our contemporaries, particularly in the face of the death of a loved one. The question continues to be relevant: "Lord, for your faithful, life is changed, not ended," sings the Church in her liturgy for the deceased. "When the body of our earthly dwelling lies in death we gain an everlasting dwelling place in heaven." Through our continued reading of, and meditating upon, the Resurrection accounts, we come by faith to understand ever more clearly the reality of the words of Jesus: "I am the resurrection and the life."

24

WERE NOT OUR HEARTS BURNING?

A most rewarding experience can be found in reading through, one after the other, the Resurrection narratives of Mark, Matthew, Luke, and John, in that order. Each evangelist has devoted the final chapter of his Gospel to the risen Jesus, excepting John, who has two such chapters. (Because John's account is somewhat extended, it is treated of elsewhere.)

Beginning with Mark has its rewards for several reasons. We quickly come to recognize a major difference between the early verses of his sixteenth chapter (verses one to eight), believed by many to be the conclusion of Mark's original text, and the remaining verses (nine to twenty), labeled in some Bibles as "the longer ending." In the earlier part Mark writes that the women "went out and fled from the tomb, seized with trembling and bewilderment. They said nothing to anyone, for they were afraid" (Mark 16:8). Just a few verses later (believed to be written by a hand other than Mark's, though still part of the canonical Gospel), Mary Magdalene is said to have gone and told Jesus' companions who were mourning and weeping (Mark 16:10).

Only Matthew's Easter account mentions an earthquake that shook the Roman guards at the tomb, impelling some of them to report matters to the chief priests. The latter instructed the guards to say that disciples of Jesus had come during the night and had stolen the body of Jesus.

Luke begins his final chapter by telling the reader about the women to whom he had made reference in the preceding chapter. There we learned that they had seen the tomb and the way Jesus' body was laid in it. "They returned and prepared spices and perfumed oils. Then they rested on the sabbath according to the commandment" (Luke 23:56). Now, in the final chapter of Luke, these same women come to the tomb with their spices and find the stone rolled away from the tomb. (In Mark, too, the stone had been rolled back when the women arrived, and in Matthew the earthquake has the effect of moving the stone.) Upon entering the tomb, the women did not find the body of Jesus, but two men in dazzling garments appeared to them (in Mark it was a young man who appeared, and in Matthew an angel who rolled back the stone at the time of the earthquake) and said: "Why do you seek the living one among the dead? He is not here, but he has been raised. Remember what he said to you while he was still in Galilee, that the Son of Man must be handed over to sinners and be crucified, and rise on the third day" (Luke 24:5-7). The women then leave the tomb area to announce these things to "the eleven and all the others." Both Mark and Matthew had identified the women by name at the outset of their accounts; Luke, on the other hand, now tells the reader that the women were Mary Magdalene, Joanna, and Mary the mother of James, and others who accompanied them. This part of Luke's account closes with Peter running to the tomb, examining it, and returning home amazed at what had happened.

Certainly the women's discovery of the empty tomb is most significant, and no one would want to suggest that for Luke it played a less important role than the account that follows. But for the regular churchgoer who time and again has heard the Emmaus story, the latter assumes an importance that seems greater than all else in Luke's account. That is understandable: the Emmaus story is of great length, and the sudden appearance of Jesus, now risen, carves a lasting impression on us as we listen to this part of Luke's Gospel.

Luke makes no apology for what may seem at first sight a sudden shift of gears as he undertakes to tell us of two disciples going to a village seven miles from Jerusalem, Emmaus. Quite naturally, they were engaged in conversation about all the things that had transpired. "And it happened that while they were conversing and debating, Jesus himself drew near and walked with them, but their eyes were prevented from recognizing him" (Luke 24:15-16). When our Savior inquired of them the topic of their discussion, they stopped, looking downcast. They in turn asked Jesus if he was the only visitor to Jerusalem who did not know of the things that had taken place. "What sort of things?" asked Jesus. The two disciples then went on to describe the various events that had befallen "Jesus the Nazarene, who was a prophet mighty in deed and word before God and all the people." They then reviewed the action of the chief priests and rulers, the crucifixion, their previous great hope, and, most recently, an account of the empty tomb.

If the story thus far has already touched our hearts we are not surprised. Yet what follows cannot but augment that feeling, as the risen Jesus undertakes to review with the two disciples the Hebrew Scriptures, emphasizing those areas that prophesied the many events that had now transpired. These verses are, in a sense, the "liturgy of the word," to be followed by the "liturgy of the sacrament," at least in format. Later generations of Christians would look many times at Luke's Emmaus account and find therein the perfect structure for the Catholic Mass, the sacrifice-sacrament instituted by Jesus at the Last Supper.

When the two disciples had finished telling the risen Lord about the events that had taken place, Jesus said to them, "Oh, how foolish you are! How slow of heart to believe all that the prophets spoke! Was it not necessary that the Messiah should suffer these things and enter into his glory?" (Luke 24:25-26). Then, beginning with Moses, continues Luke, he interpreted to them what referred to him in all the Scriptures. We may well wonder: What, in the Scriptures, would Jesus have spoken of? Would he have gone back to the early pages of Genesis? Would he have spoken of the fall of our first parents? Would he have made mention of that passage in Genesis in which God, addressing himself to the serpent, said:

> I will put enmity between you and the woman,
>> and between your offspring and hers;
> He will strike at your head,
>> while you strike at his heel.   (Genesis 3:15)

When Jesus speaks of the prophecies of the Messiah, beginning with Moses, we want to remember that "Moses" signified the entire Torah (or Law or Pentateuch) — the first five books of Sacred Scripture. Would Jesus have spoken of Noah and of the covenant sealed by God at that juncture of pre-history? Would Jesus have discussed the call of Abraham, the beginning of a new people: "I will bless you, I will make of you a name of great blessing"?

Luke tells us also that Jesus began with Moses and all the prophets, and using their testimony showed that the Messiah had to suffer and so enter into his glory. Which of the prophets would the risen Savior have cited? Perhaps the second part of Isaiah: "Here is my servant whom I uphold, my chosen one with whom I am pleased, upon whom I have put my spirit" (Isaiah 42:1). And Jesus may have made reference to another of the "Servant of the Lord" oracles found in Isaiah:

> He was spurned and avoided by men,
>> a man of suffering accustomed to infirmity,
>> one of those from whom men hide their faces,
>> spurned, and we held him in no esteem.
> Yet it was our infirmities that he bore,
>> our sufferings that he endured,
>> while we thought of him as stricken,
>> as one smitten by God and afflicted.
> But he was pierced for our offenses,
>> crushed for our sins,
>> upon him was the chastisement that makes us whole,
>> by his stripes we were healed.   (Isaiah 53:30-35)

We cannot know, of course, precisely what texts our Savior singled out to discuss with the two disciples; but we do know that later, once the identity of the Risen One is recognized, they could but say: "Were not our hearts burning within us while he spoke to us on the way and opened the Scriptures to us?" (Luke 24:32). To hear Jesus speak through the Scriptures! This it was that animated the hearts of the two disciples, and this it is that must animate our hearts also. But we are not walking to Emmaus, someone may say. True, but we are on a journey on which the risen Jesus is very much walking with us. How do we hear him? By focusing on the Scriptures and allowing the Spirit of the risen Lord to speak to us, to explain to us, to open to us the deep meaning that the Scriptures have, meanings which often remain hidden simply because we are not ready to listen, not willing to give the Spirit of Jesus the opportunity to let our hearts burn.

It is in the breaking of the bread at Emmaus that the two companions recognize the risen Lord — and then he is gone from them. But all is not over: they hurry back to Jerusalem to relate to the others what they have experienced, and in the midst of their dialog with the eleven and those gathered with the eleven the Risen One again stands among them. "Peace be with you," he said. "Why are you troubled? And why do questions arise in your hearts?" He assures them that he is not a ghost, but the same loving Savior they had known and walked and talked with many times over. A further reference is made to Moses and the prophets: "You are witnesses of these things."

Luke's story will not conclude with the end of his Gospel, for a second book will follow, the Acts of the Apostles. As the Gospel comes to a close, Jesus "parted from them and was taken up into heaven." For Luke that is far too brief an account of a great event. The reader waits patiently for the beginning of Acts, where the glorification or ascension of him who burns our hearts will be more completely described.

25

I WILL BE THEIR SHEPHERD

As Saint Luke comes to the final section of his Gospel, he narrates ever so briefly the ascension of the Lord Jesus: "Then he led them out as far as Bethany, raised his hands and blessed them. As he blessed them he parted from them and was taken up to heaven" (Luke 24:50-51). But when we come to Saint Luke's second book, the Acts of the Apostles, a far more extended account of the ascension is at hand.

> When they had gathered together they asked him, "Lord, are you at this time going to restore the kingdom to Israel?" He answered them, "It is not for you to know the times or seasons that the Father has established by his own authority. But you will receive power when the Holy Spirit comes upon you, and you will be my witnesses in Jerusalem, throughout Judea and Samaria, and to the ends of the earth." When he had said this, as they were looking on, he was lifted up, and a cloud took him from their sight. While they were looking intently at the sky as he was going, suddenly two men dressed in white garments stood beside them. They said, "Men of Gali-

lee, why are you standing here looking at the sky? This
Jesus, who has been taken up from you into heaven will
return in the same way as you have seen him going into
heaven."   (Acts 1:6-11)

As in the Gospel of Luke, so here in Acts the author wishes
us to perceive events in a chronological order. The final part of the
Gospel narrates the events of the Passion of Jesus in detail, and then
moves on to the burial. Recall that those events are followed by a
lengthy resurrection narrative, with the Gospel concluding, as indicated above, by a brief description of the ascension of Jesus. Now,
in Acts, the ascension has been described, and Luke moves on to
speak of the election of a twelfth apostle to replace Judas Iscariot,
and follows that up quickly with a description of the coming of
God's Holy Spirit. "If I do not go," Jesus had said, "my Spirit will
not come; but if I go, I will send him to you." Luke would have us
see the implementation of Jesus' promise in the second chapter of
Acts.

The effect of the Spirit's coming was dramatic: the apostles
began to speak in different tongues and a large crowd that assembled
were amazed because "each one heard them speaking in his own
language." In response to those who scoffed, accusing the apostles
of having had too much new wine, Peter stood up with the other
apostles and spoke:

These people are not drunk, as you suppose, for it is only
nine o'clock in the morning. No, this is what was spoken through the prophet Joel: "It will come to pass in
the last days," God says, "that I will pour my spirit upon
all flesh. Your sons and your daughters shall prophesy,
your young men shall see visions, and your old men

dream dreams. Indeed, upon my servants and my handmaids I will pour out a portion of my spirit in those days, and they shall prophesy." (Acts 2:15-18)

When Saint Peter uses the word "prophesy," he takes us back not simply to the prophet Joel (the prophecy of Joel was composed about 400 B.C.E.), but to a whole tradition in the history of Israel that was of great importance to the Chosen People. We think, for example, of the court prophet Nathan coming to King David after the latter's twofold sin of adultery and murder, and pointing out to the king that he had sinned most seriously. Later, in the time of David's son Solomon, we recall the prophet Ahijah meeting Jeroboam, who will become the first king of the northern kingdom of Israel (about to be separated from the unified kingdom over which Saul, David and Solomon had reigned), with Ahijah wearing a new cloak. He took off his cloak, tore it into twelve pieces, and said to Jeroboam: "Take ten pieces for yourself for the Lord, the God of Israel, says: 'I will tear away the kingdom from Solomon's grasp and will give you ten of the tribes'" (1 Kings 11:30-31).

In telling the people gathered in Jerusalem on that first Christian Pentecost that Joel's prophecy is now being fulfilled, Peter foresees the role that is to come to those who embrace the Way of Jesus: they will prophesy. To prophesy means to speak out for another, and throughout the Hebrew Scriptures the prophets speak out for God if they are genuine prophets. They had to be "sent," however, or commissioned, if you will, for the task at hand. Here in the early part of Acts Peter seems to imply that those who accept the teaching of the apostles in faith and are baptized, are about to be sent, so that they may prophesy in behalf of the newly established Church of Jesus.

A sense of history, however, must be present to the new prophets if they are to prophesy wisely and well. Neither Judaism nor Christianity is a mythical religion descended from nowhere; rather, the Scriptures emphasize over and again that God's Word has gone forth, a Word communicated by God to those who wrote the Scriptures and that that Word involved flesh and blood persons from the creation of Adam and Eve forward.

The "new prophets" were aware that one of the most disastrous experiences encountered by God's Chosen People was the Exile of 587 B.C.E., when the Babylonian armies of King Nebuchadnezzar came to Jerusalem, attacked the city, tore down the surrounding walls, damaged much of the temple built hundreds of years earlier by King Solomon, and carried off into exile countless residents of Jerusalem. Something of the pathos of the situation is reflected in the Book of Lamentations:

> Come, all you who pass by the way,
>> look and see
> Whether there is any suffering like my suffering,
>> which has been dealt me
>> When the Lord afflicted me
>> on the day of his blazing wrath.
>
> (Lamentations 1:12)

The book contains five chapters, each a lamentation in itself, and each tells forth the sad and sorrowful conditions prevailing in Jerusalem in the days following the people's deportation. The poorer residents, the reader learns, were permitted to remain behind; but a feeling of desolation pervades the book and conveys the bitterness of the exile experience for all God's Chosen People living in Jerusalem.

Why had these terrible things happened? The prophet Ezekiel is believed to have been at the gates of Jerusalem at an even earlier date, perhaps around 600 B.C.E., when Babylon first tested or probed the city to determine whether or not it could be taken. Ezekiel was taken prisoner then, many believe, and during his exile in Babylon composed the great prophecy that bears his name. As he mulled over the terrible events that had transpired, he came to believe that it was largely the poor leadership exercised by the kings in both the northern kingdom of Israel and the southern kingdom of Judah that caused the downfall, first of Samaria, capital of Israel, in 721 B.C.E., and now of Judah's capital, Jerusalem, in 587.

"Son of man, prophesy against the shepherds," he writes; "thus says the Lord God: Woe to the shepherds of Israel who have been pasturing themselves. Should not shepherds pasture sheep?" The shepherds of whom Ezekiel speaks, of course, are not people who tend flocks of sheep and goats, but the rulers of the people, chiefly the kings, who neglected the welfare of those entrusted to their care. From the first moment in which Israel asked for a king, at the time of Samuel, there was a kind of intuitive understanding that a king would, in the first place, see to the well-being of his people. But, writes Ezekiel, the kings of Israel and Judah have not taken care of their people.

> You did not strengthen the weak nor heal the sick nor bind up the injured. You did not bring back the strayed nor seek the lost, but you lorded it over them harshly and brutally. So they were scattered for lack of a shepherd, and became food for the wild beasts.
>
> (Ezekiel 34:4-5)

It is because of the failure of the shepherds, concludes Ezekiel, that the terrible fate that has now befallen Judah came about. Yet God's love for his sheep has by no means ceased: "For thus says the Lord God: I myself will look after and tend my sheep. As a shepherd tends his flock when he finds himself among his scattered sheep, so will I tend my sheep." Through the lips of the prophet the Lord promises to lead his people out from among the peoples and to gather them from foreign lands; he will bring them back to their own country and in good pastures he will pasture them.

On that birthday of the Church on which Peter addressed himself to the many listening to the teaching and preaching of the apostles, the idea of prophecy was hardly a secret: "Your sons and daughters shall prophesy," Peter told them. How could they help but realize what this meant? They would be called upon to speak out clearly in behalf of the Lord God of heaven and earth; and although the Fourth Gospel had not yet been written, the relation between what Ezekiel had written and what the Lord Jesus had shown forth could readily be understood. When our Savior (in John's Gospel) spoke of himself as a good shepherd, his language was not far from that used by Ezekiel hundreds of years earlier. Jesus speaks of the shepherd walking ahead of his sheep and of the sheep following him (John 10:4). They recognize his voice, continues Jesus, but they do not recognize the voice of strangers.

The new prophets listening to Peter had to see that as an earlier prophet, Ezekiel, had spoken out for God, emphasizing the love and care that God has for his people, so now they, if they would speak out honestly in the name of the Lord Jesus, must reflect in their words the love of God for humanity continuing in the world, reflected most perfectly in the teaching and preaching of the incarnate Word, our Lord Jesus Christ.

The Sacred Scriptures, as has been emphasized so often, are

not simply a multiplication of stories: they are the two-edged sword that reminds every age of the need to respond faithfully to the love that God expends on us, Father, Son and Holy Spirit. Do we manifest a care for those around us? Or are we like those selfish kings who fed themselves, not really caring for those with whose care they had been charged? "Your sons and daughters shall prophesy," said Peter on that memorable day, and we, baptized into the Lord Jesus, are part and parcel of that same prophetic family. Jesus is indeed the Good Shepherd, but his word will have difficulty being heard, his leadership can easily be missed, if there are not willing prophets ready to speak out for God and for the loving care spoken of by the great Ezekiel. "I will be their shepherd." Can you and I help make that a reality in our age, our day?

26

CONSENTING TO HIS EXECUTION

It has been said that the Acts of the Apostles, which follows in the New Testament immediately upon the four Gospel accounts, might well be called the Gospel of the Holy Spirit. In the Gospel accounts of Mark, Matthew, Luke, and John, the incarnate Jesus accomplished wondrous things; in the book called Acts, the Spirit of Jesus, the Holy Spirit, continues to accomplish extraordinary wonders for the early Church.

The opening chapters of Acts are dominated by the figure of Peter, constituted by the incarnate Jesus in the Gospel the rock upon which Jesus' Church is to be built. In Acts, whether it is a matter of addressing great crowds of people who stand in amazement at what is transpiring, or of curing a crippled beggar, or of standing fearlessly before the Sanhedrin, or of judging those who would defraud the Church, always it is Peter who is given prominence by Saint Luke, the author of Acts. Then, in the sixth chapter, the apostles are called upon to settle a claim made by the Hellenists in the Christian community, who complain that their widows are being neglected in the daily distribution. Anxious not to overlook the word of God in order to serve at table, the apostles commission seven reputable men, filled with the Spirit and wisdom, to carry out the necessary tasks for Hellenist widows.

One of these seven, Stephen, fell into debate with members of the so-called Synagogue of Freedmen, who stirred up others and brought Stephen before the Sanhedrin. Saint Luke provides the reader of Acts with a lengthy discourse by Stephen that leads, in the end, to Stephen's being stoned to death. "The witnesses," writes Luke, "laid down their cloaks at the feet of a young man named Saul" (Acts 7:58). Stephen, as he was being stoned, cried out, "Lord Jesus, receive my spirit." Then falling to his knees he cried out in a loud voice, "Lord, do not hold this sin against them." And when he said this, he fell asleep (Acts 7:59-60). The very next words read: "Now Saul was consenting to his execution" (Acts 8:1).

With these two brief references to Saul, Luke introduces us to a man whose history shows an influence on Christianity second only to that of Jesus Christ himself. It is a history filled with zeal and forthrightness, a history that knows vicissitudes without number. If his story begins on a note indicating a certain animus toward Christianity, it ends in a key that shows forth to the world what the presence of God's Holy Spirit in a person can accomplish.

The ninth chapter of Acts begins the narration of the history of Saul, later Paul, of Tarsus. Raised strictly as a Jew, well educated in the Torah, Saul was filled with a bitter hatred for those pursuing the Christian Way, because it appeared so inimical to all for which he stood. Armed with letters to the synagogues in Damascus that gave him authority to bring back to Jerusalem in chains any persons he found following "the Way," he began a journey that would radically change his life. En route to Damascus he fell suddenly to the ground and heard a voice that said, "Saul, Saul, why are you persecuting me?" "Who are you, sir," inquired Saul. "I am Jesus," the voice replied, "whom you are persecuting" (Acts 9:1-

5). This dramatic encounter will be related by Paul over and over again in the years ahead, and though the story is set down in print, the theme of the story never changes: Saul has been persecuting Jesus, and Jesus asks Saul why.

The great light that surrounded Saul on the occasion of his experience with Jesus blinded him temporarily, and he had to be led by others into Damascus. There, a disciple of the Way, Ananias by name, is told by the Spirit of Jesus to go to Saul, who has been chosen by the Spirit to do great things for the Way, and to suffer much. When Ananias laid his hands on Saul, the latter regained his sight and was baptized. He began at once to proclaim Jesus in the synagogues, teaching that Jesus is the Son of God. Some tried to kill him, but he escaped to Jerusalem, where Barnabas introduced him to the apostles. If in pursuing Christians Saul's speech had been bold, it was still more forthright as he battled Hellenists and others in the name of Jesus. When his fellow disciples learned that some were trying to kill Saul, they sent him on to Caesarea and Tarsus.

As exciting as Luke's account of Saul's conversion is, he does not permit it to distract him so thoroughly that he forgets all else. In the tenth chapter of Acts the focus shifts again to Peter, now called upon to speak with non-Jews — a centurion called Cornelius and his household, who gave alms generously to the Jews and who prayed to God constantly. In speaking with them Peter discovers that the Good News of Jesus is not simply for the Chosen People, but for all who listen in faith and accept baptism. The experience is vital for Peter, and indeed for the burgeoning Church, for when, at a later date, some would insist that only the children of Abraham may be accepted into the Church, Peter is able to describe his experience in the home of Cornelius and to testify to the presence of the Holy Spirit on that occasion, similar to the presence of the Spirit that the earliest Christian community had witnessed at Pentecost.

From the thirteenth chapter of Acts through to the end of the book, Saint Luke's focus is clearly on Saul, now called Paul. Not surprisingly, much of the development of the early Church outside Jerusalem takes place through the Church's missionary activity, and Paul is central in that endeavor — not single-handedly, of course, but his presence is dominant, if we accept Luke's description. Further, Luke indicates as the story progresses that he is himself a companion of Paul, adding interest to a story that is already bubbling over with excitement as Paul keeps witnessing, in season and out, before kings and emperors. It is difficult to imagine a more intriguing story than that which accompanies Paul through these several chapters of Acts.

What makes the account of Saul's change to Paul so fascinating? No matter how often we hear or read the story, always there is present that sense of deep satisfaction that he who was so ready a persecutor of the Way is now zealously battling on the side of the Risen Jesus. The attractiveness of the story, I suggest, is this: it is the story of ourselves told in a different way. Not because we have persecuted the Church of Jesus Christ in precisely the way that Saul did, but because we recognize in him that *metanoia*, that change of heart, that conversion that has taken place in ourselves so often when we have been touched by the grace of God and when we have responded positively.

As the new disciple of Jesus continues on his way through Acts, we see him evangelizing in Asia Minor, accepting rejection in some instances and persecution here and there, but never a letdown in the fervor with which he has been graced from the moment of his conversion. Never again will Jesus have to say to him, "Saul, Saul, why do you persecute me?" Paul is astute, too: when imprisoned and threatened with the lash, he asks his captors if it is customary there to beat Roman citizens without trial. They are dumbfounded to learn that he enjoys Roman citizenship; he explains that as a citizen of Tarsus, no mean city, he has enjoyed Roman citizenship from birth. When an angry mob is ready to do away with him, he begins to speak to them in Hebrew, and they are amazed to discover that he knows the traditional language of the Chosen People. When his nephew informs him that there is a plot afoot to kill Paul secretly, Paul dispatches his nephew to the Roman commander who has him in custody with instructions that no one except the commander is to be told of the plot. When in Athens he discovers an inscription "to the unknown god," he tells his listeners that he is there to reveal to them who that unknown god is.

Brought to Caesarea for his own safekeeping, he speaks out before the governor, Felix, before Felix's successor, Porcius Festus, and before King Agrippa and his wife, Bernice. Throughout his testimony he maintains that he has in no way infringed the law; but because he realizes that those pressing charges will in all likelihood trump up some kind of false accusation to level against him, he appeals finally to Caesar. This leads to a journey by ship that brings all kinds of hardships to everyone aboard and that winds up in shipwreck at the island of Malta. But the Spirit of God never leaves Paul: he is confident that the testimony he has given — witness to the Risen Jesus — will bring him safely to Rome, where he hopes to place his cause at the feet of the Roman emperor.

Luke's account of Paul ends shortly after the Apostle arrives in Rome, and the reader is left without the testimony of revelation concerning Paul's end. Tradition has it that both he and Peter were martyred in Rome and that both are buried there beneath the basilicas of Saint Peter and Saint Paul. "He remained for two full years in his lodgings," writes Luke; "He received all who came to him, and with complete assurance and without hindrance he proclaimed the kingdom of God and taught about the Lord Jesus Christ" (Acts 28:30-31). By God's ineffable grace he who had consented to the execution of Stephen had by now become a most renowned witness to the Risen Jesus.